Devotions
* Ages 2-5 *

MW00768746

God
AND
Me!®

Devotions for Girls
* Ages 2-5 *

God
AND
Me!®

Lynn Marie-Ittner Klammer

ROSEKiDZ®

An imprint of Rose Publishing, Inc.
Carson, CA
www.Rose-Publishing.com

This book is lovingly dedicated to God's greatest blessings in my life:
Mark, Matthew, Leahana, Sarah and Rachel; and for Fritz — a promise kept.

GOD AND ME!® FOR AGES 2-5
©2014 by Lynn Marie-Ittner Klammer
ISBN 10: 1-885358-61-X
ISBN13: 978-1-885358-61-5
RoseKidz® reorder #L46821
JUVENILE NONFICTION/Religion/Devotion & Prayer

RoseKidz®
An imprint of Rose Publishing, Inc.
17909 Adria Maru Lane
Carson, CA 90746
www.Rose-Publishing.com

Cover Illustrator: Chuck Galey
Interior Illustrator: Aline L. Heiser

Unless otherwise noted, Scriptures are from the *Holy Bible: New International Version* (North American Edition), copyright ©1973, 1978, 1984 by the International Bible Society. Used by permission of Zondervan Bible Publishers.

Printed in South Korea   28   04.2016.APC

Table of Contents

Table of Contents

Introduction

From my house to yours I present you with 108 true stories taken from my "routine" day-to-day life as a parent. The names of the children have been changed to keep the stories interesting, but they are actually true situations from my experiences with my own four children.

Each story in *God and Me!* includes a matching set of questions, a prayer and an activity that you can do with your daughter. Through the stories depicted in these pages, you will be able to use my everyday parenting experiences to teach your little girl the Christ-centered principles that are so critical to her development and happiness. There is no set order to these devotions, and they vary in length and complexity. I purposely designed it that way so you can choose the particular devotion/activity that you have the time (or need) for each day. Some of the stories may make you happy or sad, and some may even cause you to cringe, but whatever your reaction I hope you will come away with a feeling that these profoundly wonderful, silly, mischievous and sometimes frustrating blessings of ours are truly the miracles of our lives, and that in every situation we encounter with them, there is something to be learned for all of us.

As I'm writing this introduction I'm sitting at the kitchen counter while two-year-old Sarah happily munches on a peanut butter sandwich in her uniquely adorable manner. I can never help but marvel at how fascinating my children are to me even when they're doing the most mundane things. I have to wonder: Will I still watch them with such wonder and sense of awe when they are ten, eighteen or twenty-two years old? Will they still be as entrancing, as full of that magical quality that sparkles in their eyes and warms my heart when they're no longer preschool age? I suppose I'll have to wait for my answer. Until then, I plan to bask in every mirthful giggle, absorb each soft snuggle and revel in every enchanting story that unfolds before me. And most of all, I will always and forever be eternally grateful to our Lord for the incredible blessings He has given me. May this book enhance your own sense of awe and gratitude for the miracles in your life.

I Am God's Child

Selfishness

Selfish behavior hurts everyone.
Look not only to your own interests.
~Philippians 2:4

Selfishness Satisfies No One

The pancakes smelled wonderful! They were Sarah's favorite kind — cinnamon, nutmeg, and oh, so sweet. She couldn't wait to eat some. She stood in front of the stove where her mom stood cooking and wondered how long it would be until they were done. Sarah's cousin Steven was anxiously waiting for pancakes, too. They were especially excited because eating was one of their favorite things to do together.

Finally, the long wait was over and Mom placed a big plate of pancakes on the table. Sarah took one, but when Steven reached for one also, Sarah pulled the plate away and said "me." She didn't want to share. Sarah selfishly kept all of the pancakes for herself, so Steven left the table and went off by himself to play. Sarah happily bit into a pancake…but the pancakes didn't taste so sweet today. She looked sadly across the table at where Steven usually sat and wondered where he was. Eating special, spice pancakes wasn't nearly as much fun without Steven.

Have you ever been selfish about something only to learn that being selfish has spoiled your fun? Being selfish doesn't get you more — it gets you less. When you are selfish you don't only cheat others out of something, you also cheat yourself.

Jesus doesn't want you to be selfish. He wants you to be loving and kind, sharing what you have and who you are with others, just as He shared Himself with the world.

Your Turn

1. Can you remember a time when you were selfish?
2. Why do you think people do selfish things?
3. Does Jesus like it when you are selfish?

_____

_____

_____

_____

Prayer

Help me, Jesus, to remember that selfishness hurts everyone. Thank You for teaching me how to be kind and helpful to others. Amen.

Pancakes to Share

Read this to your child: "Jesus shared Himself with everyone. He wants you to share all that you have with others. Here are some pancakes that are so good you will want to share them." Children love to cook and it's so educational, too. Here's a pancake recipe that's sure to please. These pancakes are also sweet enough that the kids won't need syrup on them, so you won't have to contend with that sticky goo all over your table, their hair, clothes, etc.

Mama's Spice Pancakes

2 eggs
2 cups flour (all-purpose)
1 cup milk
4 tablespoons canola or vegetable oil
6 teaspoons baking powder
1 teaspoon salt
3 tablespoons sugar
1 cup applesauce
pinch of ginger
1 teaspoon cinnamon
1/2 teaspoon ground cloves
1/4 teaspoon ground nutmeg

Mix all ingredients together. Use a paper towel dipped in vegetable oil to coat the bottom of a large skillet. Heat a skillet over medium heat. Flip the pancakes when first side begins to look bubbly. Serve hot. Feeds four starving children under the age of 6.

Rest

Jesus wants me to take good care of myself.
Those who hope in the Lord will renew their strength.
~Isaiah 40:31

Sick of Rest

"Am I going to miss the party?" Ann asked sadly. It was Thanksgiving day, and even though she had a fever of 105 degrees, she still wanted to go to Grandma's party.

"You're very sick, Ann," answered Mom as she pressed her cool hand to Ann's forehead. "I don't think you're well enough to go anywhere."
"But I don't want to miss Thanksgiving," pleaded Ann.

"You can't 'miss' Thanksgiving, Ann," Mom explained. "The important thing about Thanksgiving is that we thank Jesus for all He's given us. That's what's important, not the party."

"But I want to go to the party too!" said Ann.

"Going to a party isn't more important than your health," said Mom, measuring out a dose of medicine. "If you stay home today, you'll miss the party but you'll probably get better faster."

Ann didn't want to swallow her medicine, but she did anyway. She thought about what Mom had said, but she still wanted to go to the party.

"Please let me go to the party," Ann pleaded. "I'm sick of resting. I promise I'll rest tomorrow."

"I'm sorry, Ann," said Mom, "but you're body is telling us that you need to rest now, not tomorrow."

Ann was sad that she had to miss Grandma's Thanksgiving day party, but because she stayed home and rested, she was soon healthy again.

Sometimes you need to rest. Even though you would rather be doing something fun, your body needs to be still at times. Jesus expects you to take good care of your body, and keep it healthy. Ann didn't want to miss all the fun, but she did the right thing by taking good care of herself. You should do the same.

Your Turn

1. Why did Ann have to miss Grandma's Thanksgiving day party?
2. Why is it important to rest sometimes and take good care of yourself?
3. Can you remember the last time you were sick?

Prayer

Dear Jesus, I know I need to rest sometimes, even though I'd rather be playing. Thank You for having my body tell me when I need to rest, and please help me to listen. Amen.

Stay Healthy

Read this to your child: "Jesus wants you to rest and take good care of yourself. Here are some things that help make people well when they are sick. Circle the most important one, and then color the pictures. Why did you choose the one you did as most important?"

Self-Respect

You should not allow others to treat you badly.
In the name of the Lord I cut them off.
~Psalm 118:12

Abigail Does a Mean Thing

"I'm not going to play with you anymore, Abigail," said Keith to his little sister. Abigail had been throwing wooden blocks and stuffed animals at him. He had told her several times that she was wrong to throw toys at him, but Abigail just kept doing it.

"Come and play, Keith," called Abigail from upstairs. "I'll be good."

Keith decided to give Abigail a second chance and went back up to her room to play. Minutes later, however, Abigail was once again throwing toys. "That's it," said Keith. "I'm never playing with you again."

Keith went into his own room and closed the door. For the rest of the day he played by himself.

Sometimes people are mean to you or say bad things about you. It's important that you remember how wonderful you really are and how much Jesus loves you — that's what "self-respect" is all about. If you remember that, then it will be easier to protect yourself from bad things. Keith had enough self-respect to not allow himself to be treated badly by Abigail. He knew that Jesus wouldn't want him to be treated that way, so he didn't play with Abigail until she stopped throwing toys at him.

Your Turn

1. What did Abigail do that was mean to Keith?
2. Was it a good thing that Keith didn't play with Abigail anymore? Why or why not?
3. Can you remember a time when someone was mean to you? How did you handle it?

_____

_____

_____

_____

_____

Prayer

Thank You, Jesus, for teaching me that I'm a wonderful person. Help me to never allow others to treat me badly. Amen.

Find the Different Toy

Read this to your child: "Jesus loves you and wants people to be nice to you, but sometimes people are mean anyway. Here are some of the toys Abigail was throwing at Keith. Color the picture in each row that is different from the others in that row."

Answers are on page 235.

Anticipation

Sometimes waiting for something is half the fun.
Blessed is the one who waits.
~Daniel 12:12

The Fun of Waiting

Bobbie had waited and waited until she just couldn't stand to wait any longer. When would it happen? When would her tooth finally come out?

It had been loose for weeks. Each day she carefully wiggled it back and forth with her finger, and each day it got looser. Every day she showed her loose tooth to her mom and they discussed how she'd soon get a brand new tooth in place of her old one, and how the tooth fairy would give her a dollar bill for the old tooth.

One night, as Bobbie was getting ready for bed, the tooth seemed extra loose. Bobbie wiggled it and wiggled it, and pop, it came out. She was so happy! She ran to Mom and Daddy with her tooth in her hand, and after many hugs and smiles, they put the tooth under Bobbie's pillow for the tooth fairy.

In the morning, Bobbie awoke to find a dollar bill under her pillow where the tooth had been. She was happy to have another dollar to save, but also a little sad. It had been so exciting to feel her loose tooth each day and dream of the day that it would come out. Now she didn't have anything to look forward to anymore.

Have you ever wanted something a whole lot, and then found out that getting what you wanted wasn't nearly as much fun as waiting for it? Sometimes waiting for something is as much of a gift as the gift itself.

Your Turn

1. Why did Bobbie want her tooth to come out?
2. Why was Bobbie sad after her tooth came out?
3. Can you remember a time when waiting for something was a lot of fun (perhaps a birthday or Christmas)?

_____

_____

_____

_____

Prayer

Thank You, Jesus, for all of Your gifts — even the gift of anticipation, which makes waiting for something so much fun. Amen.

Things Worth Waiting For

Read this to your child: "The Bible teaches 'Blessed is the one who waits.' Color these pictures of things that are fun to wait for."

"Now draw your own picture of something you like waiting for."

Choices

Don't just do what feels good. Do what is good.
He will instruct him in the way chosen for him.

~Psalm 25:12

Making Good Choices

Patty had a difficult choice to make. She had only three dollars to spend, but two things that she wanted to buy.

The first thing Patty wanted was a box of chocolates. They were filled with caramel and nougat and covered with smooth, sweet dark chocolate. As she looked at the candy on the store shelf, she could almost taste it.

The second thing that Patty wanted was a brand-new book. The picture on the cover showed a volcano erupting with black smoke billowing up into the sky, and bright red lava flowing down the sides of the mountain. It looked very exciting.

Patty wanted both the box of candy and the book, but since she only had enough money for one, how could she decide? After a lot of thought, Patty finally reached a decision. Can you guess which one she chose?

Patty decided to buy the book. The candy would have tasted wonderful, but once eaten, would have been gone forever. The book, however, could be read and enjoyed over and over again, and she would also learn something from it.

Jesus teaches to not just do what feels good, but instead to do what is good. Making choices can be a lot easier if you think beyond how you feel right now, and instead think about how things will affect you tomorrow and the next day.

Your Turn

1. Why was Patty's decision so hard to make?
2. Why did Patty finally choose to buy the book instead of the chocolates?
3. Can you remember a time when you had a difficult choice to make?

_____

_____

_____

_____

Prayer

Jesus, please help me to make choices that are not only good, but good for me as well. Amen.

Choices

Read this to your child: "Jesus wants you to do right, not just what feels right at the moment. Just like Patty did, you must think carefully before you make a choice. Color Patty's two choices."

"Now color these two choices. Which one would you choose?"

 # Caution

Jesus wants me to be careful and take good care of myself.
A fool is reckless.
~Proverbs 14:16

Be Careful

"Hi, Mom," Elizabeth's voice called out. Mom looked around, but didn't see her. Mom had come outside to help Daddy with the shed he was building. He had just finished putting the roof on, and needed help putting up the doors.

"Up here, Mom," Elizabeth called again. Mom looked up to see Elizabeth in the attic of the shed. Daddy hadn't put the doors on the attic yet, so there was a big hole where Elizabeth could see outside. Elizabeth was hanging over the edge with a huge grin on her face.

Mom was worried about Elizabeth because she wasn't sure Elizabeth understood how easy it would be to fall out of the attic. "Be careful, Elizabeth," Mom called up to her. "You're a long way up there. If you fall you might get hurt."

Elizabeth slowly backed away from the attic ledge. She knew what Mom said was true. Even though it was fun to hang over the side, it was too dangerous.

Lots of things can seem like fun, but are far too dangerous to actually do. You must always be careful, no matter what you are doing. The life Jesus has given you is precious. He takes good care of you, but expects you to also take good care of yourself.

Your Turn

1. Was Elizabeth being careful?
2. Why should you always be careful?
3. What happened the last time that you weren't careful enough?

_____

_____

_____

_____

_____

Prayer

Thank You, Jesus, for taking such good care of me. Please help me to take good care of myself as well. Amen.

Stay Safe!

Read this to your child: "Jesus has given You the precious gift of life. You must do your best to protect that life. Draw an X through the pictures that show something too dangerous to do. Color the one that looks safe."

Answers are on page 235.

Promises

You must never break your promises.
When a man makes a vow...he must not break his word.
~Numbers 30:2

God's Promise

Jack and Helen love the story of Noah's ark. From the time when they were very little, Mom would read in the Bible how God sent a big flood that covered the whole world. Only Noah's family and two of each kind of animal were put in the ark to live through the flood.

Jack and Helen were scared the first time they heard the story of Noah's ark. They were afraid that God might send another flood to cover the earth. What if water covered everything and they didn't have an ark to escape in? What would happen to their house, their toys and all their friends? Mom explained to Jack and Helen that after the great flood, God promised He would never again cover the entire earth with water: "Never again will I destroy all living creatures" (Genesis 8:21).

You don't have to worry that God will send another great flood because you know that God would never, ever break a promise. God is always honest and always keeps His promises, so you can trust everything He tells you.

You should follow God's example by keeping your promises as well. If you never make a promise unless you're sure you can keep it, people will know that you are good and honest, and what you say will be trusted.

Your Turn

1. What happened to Noah and his family?
2. Why were Jack and Helen scared the first time they heard the story of Noah's ark?
3. Why should Jack and Helen not be afraid?

_____

_____

_____

_____

_____

Prayer

Thank You, Jesus, for teaching me about promises. Please help me to always keep the promises I make. Amen.

Make Your Own Flood

Read this to your child: "The story of Noah's ark is a reminder of how important a promise is. God keeps His promises. You should keep yours." This activity is certain to make a lasting impression on your child. You can recreate the great flood in your own bathtub!

What You Need
- bathtub
- toy boat or anything that will float
- bowl

What to Do

Invert a non-plastic bowl in the center of the bathtub with your "ark" on top of it. Close the drain and start the water running. As the water rises, it will slowly rise to cover the bowl and the "ark" will float away—just like Noah's ark in the great flood.

Note: We use a toy boat to represent Noah's ark, but you could use anything that will float—a foam cup, a sponge, a cork, etc.

Acceptance

No matter what you do, Jesus loves and accepts you.
*Nor anything else in all creation, will be able to
separate us from the love of God.*

~Romans 8:39

Gumball Temptation

Ronnie was told that she could only have one piece of gum. It was almost dinner time, and Mom and Daddy didn't want her to be too full of candy to eat her supper.

Ronnie went to the canister where Mom kept the gum balls. They all looked so good she couldn't decide on just one. There were red ones, and blue ones, yellow and green. There were white ones, too, but Ronnie didn't like those. What a hard decision!

A few minutes later Daddy noticed that Ronnie looked like she had more than one gum ball in her mouth. "Did you take more than one piece of gum?" Daddy asked. Ronnie looked scared, and she felt guilty as she answered "No, I just took one."

When Daddy told Ronnie to open her mouth, however, the truth was obvious. There in her mouth Daddy could see both green and yellow gum. Not only had Ronnie disobeyed her parents, she had also lied about it.

Ronnie knew she had done a bad thing. She cried and cried, and said over and over again that she was sorry. She knew that Jesus doesn't like when she disobeys her parents or lies. She was worried that Jesus wouldn't like her anymore.

Ronnie should have known that no matter how bad you are, if you are sorry and ask Jesus to forgive you, He will. Jesus accepts you as you are, with all of the bad things about you as well as the good ones. He helps you to be better every day.

Your Turn

1. What two things did Ronnie do that were wrong?
2. Was Ronnie sorry for what she had done?
3. Does Jesus still accept you even when you do bad things?

_____

_____

_____

_____

Prayer

Thank You, Jesus, for accepting me as I am, for understanding when I do wrong, and forgiving me when I'm sorry. Amen.

Healthy Snacks

Read this to your child: "Jesus accepts you as you are but He wants you to do your best to be good."

What You Need
- cookie cutters
- bread
- peanut butter, jam or some other filling

What to Do
Read this to your child: "Perhaps Ronnie could have avoided temptation better if she had snacked on a healthy food instead of gumballs. Make a sandwich with your favorite things and then use cookie cutters to cut the sandwich into fun shapes. You can eat the scraps or throw them outside for the birds. Here is a picture for you to color when you are done."

Beauty

True beauty comes from who you are, not what you look like.
Your beauty should not come from outward adornment...
it should be that of your inner self.

~1 Peter 3:3-4

True Beauty

Ivy loves jewelry. She has pretty pearl necklaces, little silver rings, tiny gold earrings and bracelets of every color. She keeps all of her treasures in a beautiful pink and white jewelry box that her Aunt Leah gave her. She takes them out to wear on special occasions.

One Sunday, as Ivy was getting dressed for church, Mom told her to pick out a necklace to wear. As Ivy sorted through all of her fancy jewelry she found it hard to decide on just one. When she finally told Mom she was ready, Mom couldn't believe her eyes! Ivy was wearing every piece of jewelry she had. She was covered in necklaces and bracelets, and every one of her fingers had a ring on it. Mom asked Ivy why she had put on all of her jewelry and Ivy answered, "Because I want to be pretty for Jesus."

Just like Ivy, you may sometimes forget that what you look like on the outside isn't as important as who you are on the inside. True beauty comes from who you are, not what you look like. Jesus loves you and thinks you're beautiful, no matter what you're wearing.

Your Turn

1. Why did Ivy put on all of her jewelry?
2. Does Jesus love you more if you wear fancy clothes and jewelry?
3. What's the difference between being pretty on the outside and the inside?

_____

_____

_____

_____

Prayer

Jesus, I want to always be beautiful for You. Help me to be honest, loving and all of the other good things that make me pretty on the inside. Amen.

Macaroni Necklace & Bracelet

Read this to your child: "Sometimes it is fun to dress fancy as long as you remember that it is what you are like on the inside that counts. Jesus thinks you are pretty no matter what you are wearing."

What You Need
• string or yarn
• macaroni

What to Do
Help your child lace different sizes and shapes of macaroni on a piece of string or yarn. Tie the ends together after the desired length is reached.

Note: You can also use buttons, beads or anything else you have around the house that is light and has a hole in it for the string to pass through.

Self-Care

You can't help others if you don't take good care of yourself first.
Be careful, or your hearts will be weighed
down with...the anxieties of life.

~Luke 21:34

Hurry, Hurry!

"Hurry, hurry! Let's go!" Mom called as she shooed the children to the door. Joshua and baby Samantha had an appointment and she was taking the other children to Grandma's. They had over-slept and were running late.

Mom quickly put on the children's shoes and coats, grabbed the diaper bag, and hurried them out to the van.

Finally everyone was in the van and they were on their way to Grandma's house. They were about five minutes down the road when Chelsea asked, "Why are you wearing your garden shoes, Mom?" Mom looked down and saw that she was wearing her old, muddy garden shoes. She didn't have any socks on either. She had been so busy getting everyone else ready that she had forgotten to put her socks and shoes on. Mom hurried back home to get her shoes, but she was then late for the appointment.

Sometimes you may get so busy taking care of others that you forget to take care of yourself. Jesus wants you to help other people, but you must remember that you can't do as much good for others if you aren't healthy and happy yourself. If you take time to care for yourself, you will have more time and energy to care for others.

Your Turn

1. What did Mom leave home without?
2. Why do you think Mom forgot her socks and shoes?
3. Have you ever forgotten something that you needed for yourself because you were so busy helping someone else?

_____

_____

_____

_____

Prayer

Thank You, Jesus, for giving me the ability to help others, but please help me to remember to also take good care of myself. Amen.

Star Show

Read this to your child: "Jesus wants you to take good care of yourself and enjoy the life He has given you. When you get too busy, you may often forget the simple things in life—like how good the warm sun feels shining on your face or the beauty of the twinkling stars at night. Here's a way to make your own star show."

What You Need
- piece of cardboard
- pencil
- safety scissors
- flashlight

What to Do
Draw the shapes you want on a piece of cardboard. You can use this drawing as a stencil (just poke pinholes in the cardboard) or draw the shapes you like. Cut out the shapes, then go to a dark room. Shine the flashlight at the cardboard as you hold it up in front of a wall and you will see your shape appear on the wall.

Complaining

Complaining only makes matters worse.
Do everything without complaining or arguing.
~Philippians 2:14

I Don't Want to Go to Bed!

"I don't want to go to bed," complained Ashley. "Why do I have to go to bed now?" she asked.

"You need to go to bed so you'll be able to get up on time in the morning," answered Mom.

"But I'll get up on time. I promise," pleaded Ashley. She was having a hard time understanding because she was so tired.

"If you don't go to bed now, Ashley, you'll be too tired to get up in the morning," Mom continued.

"But I don't want to go to bed. I'm not tired. I don't like it."

"Ashley," Mom said, "that's it! Go to bed NOW!" She was getting tired of Ashley's complaining.

Ashley did finally go to bed, but only after Mom was stern with her. She also didn't get a bedtime story because she had wasted so much time complaining.

Jesus doesn't like for you to complain. He says you should let everything you say be good and helpful. Complaining usually doesn't help what you are upset about, and as in Ashley's case, it can just make matters worse.

Your Turn

1. What was Ashley complaining about?
2. Did complaining get Ashley what she wanted?
3. What could Ashley have done instead of complaining?

_____

_____

_____

_____

_____

Prayer

Jesus, help me to remember that complaining isn't the way to make things better. Guide me to be good and helpful in all I do. Amen.

Puppet Play

Read this to your child: "Jesus does not like it when you complain. Instead of complaining you should talk about what is bothering you." Sometimes it is difficult for children to express their feelings to a parent. They often find it easier to communicate through play. After making this project, let the puppets talk for you. You may be surprised by how much you learn. You can either make your own puppets out of old socks or start from scratch using these directions.

What You Need
- fabric or felt
- safety scissors
- needle and thread
- decorations (buttons, beads, etc.)

What to Do
Trace the child's hand on the fabric (as if making a mitten rather than a glove). Cut out two identical pieces of fabric and stitch them together. Decorate by sewing on buttons or beads for eyes, nose, etc. You can also use various shapes of macaroni to decorate.

Tips for puppet play:
1. Give the puppets names (i.e. "mama puppet" & "Ashley puppet").
2. Start out with a neutral topic for the first 60 seconds. For example, you could say: "You are a very pretty puppet. Can you sing me a song?"
3. Slowly ease into the topic that concerns you (i.e., bedtime, eating healthy, cleaning up toys, etc.).
4. Ask your child's puppet direct questions and say as little as possible. Let your child's puppet do most of the talking. Keep the conversation on the correct topic.
5. Accept whatever your child's puppet tells you. Remember, feelings aren't "good" or "bad," they just "are". Seeing the situation from your child's perspective will be your first step in finding a solution to the conflict you are discussing.

 # Confidence

Jesus will help you through your fears.
It is better to take refuge in the Lord than to trust in man.
~Psalm 118:8

First Day Fears

Nikki's first day of school had finally arrived. She couldn't wait to go to school, meet the kids and do all of the new and exciting things that she'd heard about. Nikki got herself dressed, slid her arms through her backpack straps and waited by the door. She was ready to go, but she was still scared. "What if I don't do the right thing?" she wondered.

"What if the other kids don't like me?" she thought. There were so many things to wonder and worry about.

Mom and Daddy told Nikki that it was normal to feel scared about doing something new. They talked with her about what school would be like, and told her that they were very proud of her. Nikki felt a little better, and had a good time at school after all.

Everyone, even adults, feels unsure of themselves when they're about to do something they've never done before. You can overcome some of your worry if you just take it one step at a time, remembering that Jesus is there with you. Even when you make mistakes, or bad things happen, Jesus will never leave your side. He loves you no matter what, and you can count on Him and His teachings to guide you through anything.

Your Turn

1. Why was Nikki nervous?
2. What are some things Nikki could have done to make herself feel better?
3. When was the last time you felt nervous about something?

_____

_____

_____

_____

_____

Prayer

You are always with me, Jesus, even when I'm in a strange place, or doing something new. Help me to always remember that You will never leave me. Amen.

Make Your Own Puzzle

Read this to your child: "No matter how scared you are, or what new thing you're about to do, Jesus will be with you. He has given you family and friends to love and care for you, and He will guide you through all of your fears. You can make your own puzzle to show the wonderful things you are thankful for in your life. Just draw your picture on a piece of paper, and don't forget to put Jesus in the middle because He should be the center of your life. Have your mom or dad cut it out for you, then you'll have your very own puzzle! Here is one idea for a puzzle that you may color."

Confession

You should confess when you do something wrong.
Confess your sins to each other and pray for each other.

~James 5:16

Who Did It?

"Who did this?" demanded Melissa. "Who destroyed my building?"

Melissa had carefully built a tall tower out of wooden blocks. She left the room for a few minutes and when she got back the tower had been toppled over. "Vickie," Melissa asked with anger in her voice, "did you do this?" Vickie, sitting by the toy box playing with a doll, shook her head no.

"Did you do this, Jamie?" Melissa asked her little sister, but Jamie just ignored her.

"I wonder who did this?" Melissa said to herself as she set to work rebuilding her tower of blocks.

Later that day, Vickie told Mom that she had been the one who knocked Melissa's tower over. Mom told her she should tell Melissa the truth, so Vickie, with tears in her eyes, confessed to Melissa what she had done. She said she was sorry, and as they hugged, Melissa said, "It's okay, Vickie, I forgive you."

There are several reasons for confessing when you do something wrong. Not only is confessing your sin the right thing to do, it also can make you feel better. The Bible says that confession is the first step of forgiveness. If you confess and say you are sorry for what you have done wrong, you will then hopefully not make the same mistake.

Your Turn

1. What did Vickie do that was wrong?
2. Why do you think Vickie confessed her sin to Melissa?
3. Can you remember a time when you confessed something that you had done wrong?

_____

_____

_____

_____

_____

Prayer

Thank You, Jesus, for forgiving me when I confess my sins to You.
Help me to be a better person every day of my life. Amen.

Special Wrapping Paper

Read this to your child: "Jesus taught to confess sins when you do something wrong. You can ask for forgiveness by telling the person you hurt that you are sorry. Sometimes you can say you are sorry by making the person a special gift."

What You Need
- sponges
- produce
- diluted food coloring
- paper grocery bags

What to Do
Cut sponges into whatever shapes you like (some craft stores sell precut sponges). If using produce, fresh, hard apples work best, but pears or potatoes work quite well also. Slice produce horizontally for a circular shape. Pears sliced vertically will look just like a pear on paper, and so on. Help your child to dip her shape into the diluted food coloring and then stamp it onto paper. It only takes a few minutes to dry, and then you are ready to wrap a special gift with special gift wrap.

Control

You should base your choices on what Jesus teaches.
If the Lord is God, follow him.
~1 Kings 18:21

The Power to Choose

"No," Ann said. "No diaper!" Mom was holding up a diaper and telling Ann it was time for a diaper change, but Ann kept wildly shaking her head no. Mom told Ann that she was wet and needed to be changed, but Ann still said, "No!"

Then Mom had an idea. Holding up two diapers, Mom asked Ann, "Which diaper should we use?" Ann paused a moment. She seemed to be thinking about the two diapers Mom was holding up in front of her.

Suddenly, Ann pointed to the diaper on the left and laid down to be changed. Even though the two diapers were exactly the same, Ann still chose one because she finally was given the power to make a choice.

Just like Ann, you may want to have control over your life. Whether you're only as old as Ann, or Mom and Dad's age, you want to feel that you make the decisions about what is going to happen to yourself.

Jesus teaches that knowing God leads to self-control (2 Peter 1:5-8). It is good for you to make as many of your own choices as possible, as long as you base those choices on what Jesus teaches is right to do.

Your Turn

1. Why didn't Ann want her diaper changed?
2. How do you think Ann felt after getting to make her own choice about which diaper to use?
3. Is there something you wish you could decide for yourself?

_____

_____

_____

_____

_____

_____

Prayer

Help me, Jesus, to remember to make my choices based on what You teach us is right to do. Amen.

Dough Shapes

Read this to your child: "Jesus wants you to make your own choices, as long as those choices are based on His teachings. You can make your own dough, and choose to make it into anything you want to."

What You Need

- 1 1/2 cups water
- 2 tablespoons vegetable oil
- 1/2 cup salt
- 2 cups flour
- 4 tablespoons cream of tartar

What to Do

Combine all of the ingredients and stir them over medium heat until a ball forms (it will be very hard to stir). Cool and have your child help you knead the dough until it is smooth (3 to 5 minutes). Wrap the dough in plastic wrap while it is still warm and allow it to cool. Store the dough in the refrigerator in a plastic container. It can be used over and over again.

Note: This dough is not for eating, only for play. You can use food coloring to tint your dough if you like, but only use the kind that won't stain clothes or counter tops.

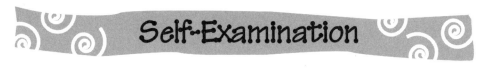

Self-Examination

You should think more about your own sins than the sins of others.
If any one of you is without sin, let him
be the first to throw a stone at her.

~John 8:7

Who Is More Naughty?

"You left your cup out, Henry," reminded Peggy. "You're naughty!"

Henry had left his cup with milk in it on the coffee table and little Kim had spilled it on the living room rug.

"I am not naughty," insisted Henry. "It was an accident, Peggy. I just forgot."

He and Peggy always sat in the living room each morning with their cup of milk as they watched TV. Henry knew that it was an important rule that no food should be left out. If a cup were left out, little Kim or baby Katie could get it and make a big mess.

"Naughty, naughty," Peggy continued to tease. "You're a bad, bad boy."

Peggy was having a lot of fun scolding Henry. In fact, she was having so much fun that she forgot that her own cup was still on the table. In a matter of moments, Kim had grabbed Peggy's cup and dumped it on the floor as well. If Peggy had paid more attention to following the rules herself, instead of picking on Henry, her cup would have never been spilled.

Everyone does bad things sometimes. Instead of talking about what others have done wrong, you should think about your own mistakes and try to do better. It can sometimes be good to remind others of their sins, but you must pay attention to your own choices in life. Jesus wants you to work on being the best you can be, no matter what other people are doing.

Your Turn

1. Was Henry the only person who was naughty?
2. Why shouldn't you be critical of others?
3. Are there some things you could do better?

_____

_____

_____

Prayer

Please help me, Jesus, to work on being a better person myself,
instead of thinking about what other people are doing wrong. Amen.

Help Peggy Put Her Cup Away!

Read this to your child: "Jesus wants you to do the right thing even if other people are not. Peggy forgot that. Can you help Peggy find her way to the refrigerator so she can put her cup away?"

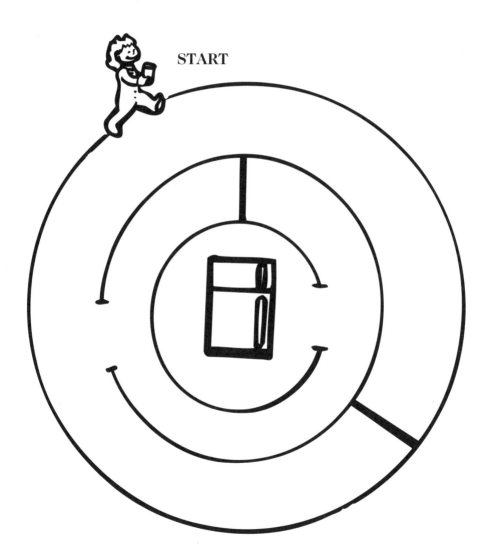

START

Answer is on page 235.

Habits

Replace your bad habits with good ones.
Set your minds on things above.

~Colossians 3:2

Bad Habits Are Hard to Break

Cindy would not stop biting her nails. Mom explained to her that nails do not look pretty if the edges are bitten, but Cindy chewed on them anyway.

She didn't just chew her fingernails either—Cindy chewed her toenails, too.

Sometimes she chewed her nails so much that they split and bled. It was a very bad habit.

Mom told Cindy that if she stopped chewing on her nails, she would give her extra hugs and kisses, but Cindy chewed her nails anyway. Then Mom told Cindy she could have a special treat if she stopped biting her nails, but Cindy still chewed them. Then Mom said she'd let Cindy stay up a little later at night for each day she left her nails alone. Cindy stopped biting her nails for a few days, but then just couldn't resist any longer. She started to bite her nails again.

One day, Mom told Cindy that if she stopped chewing her nails, she would paint Cindy's nails with the same bright pink nail polish that she used. That did it. Finally, Cindy stopping biting her nails. She loved having her nails painted with pretty pink polish even more than she liked chewing on them. After that day, Cindy always had the prettiest nails in the family, and she never chewed on them again.

Habits can be good or bad. Cindy was able to replace a bad habit with a good one. Now instead of hurting her nails by biting them she takes good care of them. Jesus likes when you take care of yourself and others, and stop any bad habits that are hurtful. You should try your best to replace any bad habits you have with good ones.

Your Turn

1. What was Cindy's bad habit?
2. What good habit did Cindy replace her bad one with?
3. Do you have any bad habits that you need to change?

_____

_____

_____

Prayer

Please help me, Jesus, to think about what habits I need to change. Replace them with good habits instead. Amen.

Hand Tracing

Read this to your child: "Jesus wants you to replace your bad habits with good ones, just like Cindy did. You can pretend that you have pretty pink nails just like Cindy. Place your hand on this paper, and then carefully trace around your hand. When you lift your hand back up, you'll see the shape of your hand. Now you can draw a nail on each finger and color it whatever color you like."

Priorities

Jesus and family should come first in your life.
As for me and my household, we will serve the Lord.
~Joshua 24:15

Paige's Priority

"Help me," called Mom. Gina had just vomited all over her crib and herself. Mama was carrying her to the bathroom, but the door was shut and she didn't have a free hand to open it. Paige, sitting just a few feet away playing video games, heard Mom's call for help, but didn't want to leave her game.

"Paige, please come help me," called Mom again. "Hurry, she's heavy."

Paige looked up briefly, but continued playing her game as she said, "I can't, Mom. I'm winning."

Mom finally had to order Paige to come help her. "Paige," Mom sternly said, "open the bathroom door now!" Only then did Paige finally help.

Paige had her priorities out of order. Priorities are the things that are the most important to us. In this case, Paige should have known that helping her mother and sister was much more important than playing a video game.

As you make choices about how to act or what you want, you should always think about what is most important to you. You should put Jesus first in your life, and value family and friends more than toys and games.

Your Turn

1. Why didn't Paige help her mom when she first asked her to?
2. Should Paige have helped her mom even though it would cause her to lose her game?
3. What is most important in your life?

_____

_____

_____

_____

_____

_____

Prayer

Please help me, Jesus, to always remember that my faith in You, and love of my family, are more important than toys and games. Amen.

Choosing Priorities

Read this to your child: "Jesus teaches to put Him first in your life and to value people more than things. Look carefully at the pictures below. Which ones are most important to you? Circle your favorite one and then color all three."

Quitting

You should finish what you start.
At the proper time we will reap a harvest if we do not give up.
~Galatians 6:9

Why Aren't the Brownies Done?

"Keep going, Kasie," said Mom. "We have to add all of the ingredients if we want brownies to eat."

Kasie was adding the flour a little at a time. It was the last ingredient, but she was getting tired. "Keep stirring, Kasie," said Mom. Kasie kept stirring, but as she did she could hear cartoons starting on the living room TV.

"I don't feel like doing this now," Kasie said, eager to go watch cartoons.

"That's okay," Mom said, "but if you don't finish making the batter now, it will be a lot longer until we have the brownies done."

Kasie thought about how much she wanted brownies to eat, but the happy sounds of her favorite cartoons were too much to resist. "I'll finish this later, Mom, okay?" she asked.

"That's okay," said Mom. Kasie ran off to watch TV.

By the time Kasie's cartoons were over, she had forgotten all about the brownie dough and soon was busy playing with her toys. Hours later she ran to Mom and asked, "Where are the brownies?"

Mom just looked at her and said, "Brownies? What brownies? You never finished making the dough."

"But I thought you did it," cried Kasie.

"No, Kasie," explained Mom. "Making the dough was your job. If you had finished that job back when you started it, the brownies would have been done hours ago."

Once you start something, it is better to keep at it until it's done. If you quit, the job may never get done, and you may not get what you want. Kasie had to wait a long time for her brownies. There will always be a lot of fun things to do, but if you finish what you start, you will be much happier. Jesus teaches to never give up and always try to do your best.

Your Turn

1. Why was Kasie upset?
2. Why didn't Kasie finish making the brownie dough?
3. Do you remember the last time you didn't finish something you started? Why didn't you?

Prayer

Jesus, please help me to always finish what I start, and not be distracted by other things. Amen.

Finding Brownies

Read this to your child: "Just as the Bible says 'we will reap a harvest if we do not give up,' you will get what you want if you keep trying. Kasie should have known that. Kasie loves brownies! Help her find her way to the biggest one."

START

Answers are on page 235.

Greed

You should be happy with what Jesus has given you.
Do not store up for yourselves treasures on earth.

~Matthew 6:19

I Want More!

The children had gone trick-or-treating and brought home four bags full of candy. When all of the candy was emptied out into the family candy bowl, they couldn't believe how much there was! The big shiny bowl was filled with everything from lollipops to gumdrops and bubble gum.

Jake was the first to dig into the bowl for a sweet treat. He sat at the table happily munching on the biggest green gumdrop he could find as he watched Tiffany pick out her favorite items and sit down beside him. They sat at the table for quite some time, peacefully sharing their candy.

Their peaceful time was soon ended, however, when Tiffany got greedy. Even though she had more candy then she could possibly eat, she wanted more.

"Give me that!" Tiffany suddenly shouted at Jake as she grabbed for the chocolate bar he was holding in his hand.

"Tiffany, stop it," Jake said as he pushed her hand away. "You have your own candy."

"I want more!" Tiffany insisted as she reached for Jake's candy again.

When Daddy saw what was going on, he said, "Stop it, Tiffany! If you can't behave, then you can just go to bed."

Tiffany's greed didn't get her more candy. Instead, being greedy caused Tiffany to have her candy taken away for the night, and she was sent to bed. Greed is like that. When you allow yourself to want more than you need, or should have, you could lose everything instead.

Jesus has given you all that you have, and all that you need. If you trust Jesus to know what is best for you, then you wont be greedy and want more than He has provided for you. Tiffany should have been happy with what she had, and so should you.

Your Turn

1. Why was Tiffany greedy?
2. Did being greedy get Tiffany what she wanted?
3. Have you ever been greedy?

Prayer

Please help me, Jesus, to never be greedy. Thank You for everything You've given me. Amen.

Connect the Lines

Read this to your child: "Jesus gives all you need. You should never be greedy for more. Connect the broken lines to finish the picture, then color it."

Truth

What Jesus tells us is always true.
Your law is true.
~Psalm 119:142

What's True?

"Come on, come on. It's okay," said Althea in a soft, serious voice. She wanted Bea to play with her, but Bea wasn't sure she wanted to.

"It's okay, Bea," said Althea again. "This game is fun. Just hold still."

Bea held still because Althea told her they would have fun. Bea wanted to believe Althea, but so far, it didn't seem like much fun to her. One by one, Althea stuffed toys inside Bea's shirt as Bea stood perfectly still. When her shirt was filled with toys, Bea finally had enough.

"This isn't fun at all," she thought as she screamed in anger. Bea ran around the room trying to shake all the toys out of her shirt. She was mad that Althea had lied to her about this game being fun.

Sometimes the truth can be hard to figure out. What one person thinks is true may not be what another person believes. So how do you know what to believe? Whom should you listen to?

It is important to remember that there is a difference between someone's opinion and the truth. For example, one person may like the taste of apple pie, while another doesn't. So does apple pie taste good or doesn't it? It really depends on whom you are asking, doesn't it? The one Person you can always count on for the absolute truth is Jesus. What you read in the Bible about Jesus, and how He wants you to live, isn't just opinion. It is the truth.

Your Turn

1. What did Althea tell Bea?
2. Why did Bea get angry with Althea?
3. Did Althea lie to Bea, or was she just telling Bea her opinion?

_____

_____

_____

_____

_____

Prayer

Dear Jesus, thank You for the gift of your Bible. I know it is full of the truth. Amen.

Find the Truth

Read this to your child: "What Jesus teaches in the Bible is the one thing you can always believe is the truth. Find your way through the maze to the one thing you know will always be true. Be careful—don't take a wrong turn!"

START

Answer is on page 235.

God Helps Me
Get Along

Love

Real love puts others first.
As I have loved you, so you must love one another.
~John 13:34

A Greater Love

When our first baby was born we were very happy. We named our baby Matthew, after one of Jesus' disciples, because we wanted him to have a name that showed our faith in Jesus.

The day we were supposed to take Matthew home from the hospital, the doctor told us that Matthew would have to stay for a while. The doctor said that Matthew might be very sick, and they needed to watch him closely until they were sure he was OK.

At that moment, for the first time in my life, I knew that I would trade my life for another person. I prayed to God that if someone needed to die, that He take me instead of my child. I was surprised by how strong my love for Matthew was. After all, he was just a baby and only one day old. I didn't really know anything about him. How could I love someone so much that I'd trade my life for his?

After the doctor ran some tests on Matthew, we learned he was fine, and we were able to take him home.

Have you ever loved someone so much that you would rather be the one hurting than see him or her in pain? Have you ever wondered how Jesus could love you so much that He would actually die for you? It can be hard to understand, but just like moms and dads love their children more than themselves, God loves us—because we are all God's children.

Your Turn

1. How did Jesus teach Matthew's mom about love?
2. Why did Jesus die for you?
3. What can you do for others to show them how much you love them?

_____

_____

_____

_____

_____

Prayer

Thank You, God, for showing me what real love is. Help me to love others like You love me. Amen.

A Birth Tree

The miracle of your child's birth should remind you of the greatest miracle of all — Jesus' birth, His gift of Himself and His love. Jesus' love for you is everlasting, as is your love for your children. Planting a tree is a beautiful way to commemorate that love. Many people like to plant a tree when someone dies as a way to remember them, but why not plant a tree in honor of someone's birth? You may find a local organization that gives small saplings away, or you could purchase a larger one. I prefer planting a larger sapling because you can make a small mark on its trunk for each year of the child's growth. It is a special way to encourage an interest in nature as well as being a unique gift and life-long memento. Here is a tree for your child to color until you can plant the real thing.

Lying

Lying is a bad thing to do.

You shall not give false testimony against your neighbor.

~Exodus 20:16

Chester Did It!

Jennie stood in the middle of the kitchen with a pile of dolls at her feet. She was supposed to put her toys away, but she hadn't done it. Instead of doing what her mother had told her to do, she had brought even more of her dolls out into the kitchen.

When Jennie's mother walked into the kitchen, she was surprised to find that the dolls were still there. "Jennie, who brought all of these toys in here?" asked Mom.

"Chester did it!" yelled Jennie.

Mom knew that Jennie's big brother, Chester, wasn't even at home, so he couldn't have been the one to bring out the toys, and she scolded Jennie for lying about her brother.

One of the commandments that Jesus gave says that you should not bear false witness against your neighbor. This means that you shouldn't lie about other people. You should instead admit when you've done something wrong, and try to not make the same mistake again.

Your Turn

1. Why did Jennie lie?
2. Why should you never lie?
3. Do you remember a time that you lied about something?

_____

_____

_____

_____

_____

_____

_____

Prayer

Jesus, please help me to remember that lying is a bad thing. Help me to be truthful and honest every day. Amen.

I'm Sorry

Read this to your child: "Color this picture of Jennie telling Jesus how sorry she is for lying about her brother."

Sympathy

Sympathy is a special feeling of caring for others.
Finally, all of you...be sympathetic.

~1 Peter 3:8

Where's Kelsey?

When Cynthia played with Kelsey it was a special time. Cynthia showed Kelsey her toys and played with her on the living room floor while their moms sat and talked. Cynthia and Kelsey didn't get to see each other very often because they lived far apart, so they especially enjoyed their visits.

One day when Kelsey was coming to visit, Cynthia happily took out all of the toys she wanted to show her friend, but that morning Kelsey's mother called to say she couldn't come. Kelsey was very sick.

As Cynthia put away the toys that she had planned to share with Kelsey, she felt sad and missed her friend. She also felt something a little different than just sadness over missing their play date. Cynthia felt sorry for Kelsey and wished that Kelsey didn't have to be sick anymore.

What Cynthia felt for Kelsey is called "sympathy." It's a special feeling you have for someone when your concern isn't for yourself. It is when you feel sad for someone else. God likes for you to show sympathy to others because it means you love them.

Your Turn

1. Why did Cynthia feel sympathy for Kelsey?
2. Have you ever felt sympathy for someone?
3. Can you remember a time when someone might have felt sympathy for you?

_____

_____

_____

_____

_____

_____

Prayer

Jesus, thank You for giving me the wonderful feeling of sympathy that helps me to care for others. Amen.

Faces of Sympathy

Read this to your child: "Sympathy is one of the many ways Jesus gives you to show your love for others. Circle the picture that shows how Cynthia felt when Kelsey got sick. How would you feel if your friend got sick?"

Answer is on page 235.

Blame

You should never blame others for your own sins.
You are responsible for the wrong I am suffering.

~Genesis 16:5

Pointing Out Blame

Sue and her cousin Steven, both 2, knew it was against the rules to climb the stairs. Mom had told them that they were too little yet to be on the stairs by themselves, but that didn't stop them from trying to climb up anyway.

A few seconds later, Mom saw Sue and Steven climbing up the stairs and asked, "Just what do you two think you're doing?"

"Sue make me," said Steven as he angrily pointed at cousin Sue.

Sue pointed right back at Steven and said, "Steve do it." She was just as angry, and even stomped her feet as she spoke. Both kids had been caught climbing up the stairs even though they knew it was dangerous for them and against the rules, and they each blamed the other.

When you are caught doing something wrong, it can be easy to blame someone else. But even though blaming someone for your own poor choices might save you from getting punished, lying only makes your sin worse. It may have made Jesus sad when Steven and Sue broke the rules, but it make Him even more sad when they placed the blame on each other. Instead, they should have simply admitted they were wrong and said they were sorry.

Your Turn

1. What two things did Steven and Sue do that were wrong?
2. What should they have done instead?
3. Do you admit when you are wrong, or do you lie or blame someone else when you are caught?

_____

_____

_____

_____

_____

Prayer

Jesus, it's hard to admit when I've done something wrong. Please help me to never blame others for my own bad choices in life. Amen.

Stop and Think Signs

Read this to your child: "Jesus wants you to tell the truth when you do something wrong, and to never blame others. You can keep from doing bad things if you find ways to remind yourself what the rules are. A fun way to remember when something is off-limits is to put up a small sign or streamer." You can use homemade signs to help your child learn letters and numbers as well. Here's how to make a sign.

What You Need
• paper
• non-toxic crayons or marking pens
• non-toxic glitter
• safety scissors
• tape

What to Do
Here are some common shapes that should remind your child what to do. You can help your child make the signs and then post them in the places in your house where they need to be reminded to stop or be careful. You and your child can make up your own shapes, too! Your only limit is your imagination.

Signs like this are good in your house for stairways, medicine cabinets and certain off-limits cupboards.

Signs like this are good for your kitchen sink and tub.

Nurturing

You should comfort others just as Jesus comforts you.
We can comfort those...with the comfort
we have received from God.

~2 Corinthians 1:4

Sleep, Sleep Little Bear

Rebecca was very quiet. She was supposed to be asleep, but she was playing in her crib instead. She didn't know that Mom was secretly watching her through the open bedroom door.

Rebecca carefully placed her tiny, stuffed bear on the crib mattress and gently pulled the special blanket Grandma had given her up over the bear, tucking it under his furry chin. "Nap, nap," Rebecca said softly, patting the bear's tummy through the soft blanket.

Rebecca sat back and quietly watched the little bear for a moment. When the bear didn't go to sleep, Rebecca snuggled in beside him, softly whispering words of love to him as she rested her head against his. "Sleep, sleep," Rebecca said, watching and waiting for her little bear to take his nap.

Rebecca was "nurturing" her little bear. That means she was taking care of him in a kind and loving manner. Rebecca knew that taking a nap is good for your body, so she was helping her tiny bear to fall asleep happy and content.

In the same way, Jesus helps you to be healthy and happy through His kind and loving ways. Jesus stays by you so you won't be afraid, and just as Rebecca comforted her little bear, Jesus comforts you with His message of love that you can find in the Bible.

Your Turn

1. What did Rebecca's mom see her doing?
2. How does Jesus take care of you?
3. Whom do you take care of? How?

_____

_____

_____

_____

Prayer

Dear Jesus, please help me to take care of others in as warm and l ovinga way as You take care of me. Amen.

Numbers of Bears

Read this to your child: "Jesus shows you His love and nurturing in many ways. He was born, died and rose again for you. He stays by you and helps you every day and guides you to know what is right by the words in the Bible. Jesus' love for you teaches you how to love others, just as Rebecca showed her little bear her love. Here are some more little bears. Can you match each bear with its correct number? Color your favorite one."

Answer is on page 235.

Happiness

You can't find true happiness by hurting others.
Joy may end in grief.
~Proverbs 14:13

Early Morning Mischief

It was early in the morning. No one was awake yet...except for Susan. From her bed Susan could see Mom's purse, and suddenly a naughty idea popped into her head. How she would love to explore Mom's purse and all of the fun things inside it! She knew she wasn't supposed to ever go into Mom's purse, but everyone was asleep, so no one would ever know.

Carefully, quietly, Susan climbed out of bed and lowered herself to the floor. Taking Mom's purse in her hands, she pushed and pulled at the zipper. She opened it and reached inside. Many wonderful things came tumbling out. Coupons and coins, dollar bills and combs, tissues and ink pens all fell on the floor at Susan's feet. But the most wonderful thing of all was a tube of red lipstick. Oh how she loved to watch Mom put on lipstick! She pulled off the cap and began to smear some on her lips, and her cheeks, and her nose, and her arms, and before she knew it, she had red lipstick all over herself. She felt so happy...but something was wrong.

The lipstick was such a pretty color that Susan then decided to draw on the new carpet, and on the walls, and the books, and the dresser, and then she stopped. Again she felt so happy, except something was wrong. Something just didn't quite feel right. She loved playing with Mom's lipstick, but knowing that she had been naughty ruined her happiness.

Putting on her best "I'm sorry" face, Susan ran to Mom's bedroom to wake her up and tell her what she had done. Now she didn't feel happy at all. Susan just felt badly. Even fun things can make you feel badly if they are not what Jesus would want you to do. That's what happened to Susan.

Your Turn

1. Why did Susan go into Mom's purse?
2. Did you ever think it would make you happy to do something naughty?
3. How did it really make you feel?

Prayer

Jesus, please help me to remember that happiness which comes out of being naughty, or hurting others, isn't true happiness at all. Guide me to do my best each day, to do only good things. Amen.

A Spilled Maze

Read this to your child: "The best way to find happiness is by living the way Jesus tells you in the Bible. If you follow the path He has laid out for you, your life will be happy and good. Follow the trail of things from Mom's purse all the way to the tube of lipstick. Can you find your way there without making any mistakes?"

Mom's Purse

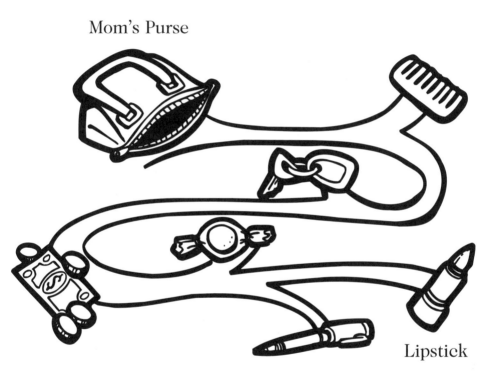

Lipstick

Answer is on page 235.

Tolerance

I should be tolerant of others.
Cry aloud for understanding.

~Proverbs 2:3

Understanding Mistakes

Anna was so mad! Every time she tried to use the phone, it wouldn't work. Anna carefully pushed the numbers that Mom told her to, but nothing happened. The phone didn't dial, and it made no sound. It was of no use at all.

One day went by, and then another. The phone didn't work for two whole days! Anna couldn't call anyone, not even Grandma or Aunt Leah, and she couldn't understand why the phone wouldn't work. Anna asked Daddy why the phone wouldn't work, and he showed her where some men were working on the road, and how they had accidentally cut the phone line. Mom said it was an accident, but Anna was still angry. Anna said, "Those workmen are idiots! They cut our phone line."

Sometimes it can be hard to understand when people make mistakes that affect you. Anna wasn't very understanding of the men who were doing the road work, but Jesus teaches that you should be tolerant of others. Just think of all of the mistakes you have made. Aren't you glad that Jesus is tolerant of you when you do the wrong thing? Aren't you glad He forgives your mistakes?

Your Turn

1. Why was Anna angry?
2. Can you remember a time when you weren't very tolerant of someone?
3. Do you think Jesus wants you to be understanding of others?

_____

_____

_____

_____

Prayer

Jesus, help me to remember to be understanding and tolerant when other people do things that I don't like. Thank You for understanding when I don't do the right thing. Amen.

Phone Fun

Read this to your child: "Jesus wants you to be tolerant of others and forgive them just as He forgives you when you make a mistake. Anna wasn't very tolerant of the men who cut her phone line. Maybe she will do better next time. Circle the picture of a telephone."

"If you could call someone on the telephone, who would it be? Draw a picture of him or her below."

Answer is on page 235.

Kindness

Be kind to other people.
Do to others what you would have them do to you.
~Matthew 7:12

Shared Rewards

Stacy knew that if she was extra good while Mom did her grocery shopping, she would get a special treat, so she was on her best behavior. She quietly walked next to Mom and carefully placed each item she gave her into the shopping cart. She never begged for candy or other things that weren't on the list, and she never, ever went so far away from Mom that she couldn't see her. When they were done shopping, Stacy got to choose a special treat. She chose a package of bubble gum. She asked Mom if she had to share it with little sister, Kathy, when they got home, and Mom said no. Special treats were only for the people who earned them.

When Stacy got home she told her sister all about the fun she had helping Mom do the shopping, and showed her the special treat. Kathy looked sad as she looked at the gum, but said nothing. Stacy quietly thought for a moment, and then she held the gum out to her sister and said, "Don't worry, Kathy. I'll share with you."

Stacy knew that Jesus wants us to treat others the same way we want people to treat us. If Kathy had been the one with the special treat, she would have wanted her to share, so she did the same for Kathy.

Your Turn

1. Why did Stacy share her gum with her sister?
2. Why should you treat people the same way you want to be treated?
3. Do you try to be kind to people all of the time?

_____

_____

_____

_____

_____

Prayer

Jesus, please help me to always remember to treat people with kindness, just as I would like to be treated. Amen.

Special Treats

Read this to your child: "Jesus gives you many special treats and He loves it when you share them with others. Color the treats below in your favorite colors. Draw a big red circle around your favorite one. Why do you like that one the best?"

Forgiveness

You should forgive others, even when they hurt you.
All the sins...will be forgiven them.

~Mark 3:28

Jessica's Sin

Billie had drawn three beautiful pictures. She had spent all day drawing them. One was a picture of pretty flowers, another had a big volcano erupting and the third one showed a campground during a lightening storm. She was very proud of her pictures.

The next day, while Billie was gone, baby Jessica crawled to where Billie's pictures were and began to play with them. She wadded the campground picture into a ball, tore the flower picture into many pieces and chewed on the volcano picture. When Billie got home and saw what her sister had done, she was very angry, and also sad. She cried, yelled and screamed at Jessica, "How could you do this?" It seemed that Billie would never be able to forgive Jessica for what she had done.

After Billie calmed down, she told Jessica (with tears still in her eyes) that what Jessica had done was wrong, but that she forgave her. Billie knew that Jesus would want her to forgive baby Jessica. She knew that Jesus forgives, no matter how bad of a thing we do. So, like Jesus, you must forgive others even when they do something that hurts you.

Your Turn

1. What did baby Jessica do that hurt Billie?
2. Why did Billie forgive Jessica?
3. When was the last time you forgave someone?

_____

_____

_____

_____

_____

Prayer

I know that You will always forgive me, Jesus. Help me to be more like You and forgive others. Amen.

Drawing Disaster

Read this to your child: "Jesus forgives you, so you must forgive others also. Billie forgave baby Jessica even though she ruined Billie's picture. Draw a line from Billie's picture to what it looked like after Jessica played with it."

Answer is on page 235.

Sharing

We should share what we have.
A generous man will himself be blessed.

~Proverbs 22:9

Guitar Wars

"I want it. Let go!" yelled Lisa as she pulled the toy guitar away from Mark. Mark chased after Lisa as she ran across the room with the guitar, and little Maggie screamed at the top of her lungs as she rolled her walker toward them both. She wanted the guitar, too.

Mom came into the room just in time to see Mark yank the guitar out of Lisa's hands. He nearly fell on Maggie in the process. Now everyone was screaming, including Mom, as she exclaimed, "That's it! If you don't take turns and share the guitar, then I'm going to take the guitar away and no one will get to play with it."

The room suddenly grew quiet. Everyone agreed to quietly share the guitar. However, moments later all three of them began to scream and fight over it again, so Mom took it away. Now the guitar was gone, and no one would get to play with it.

Because Mark, Lisa and Maggie wouldn't share their toy, none of them were able to enjoy it. Everything that you have is a gift from Jesus. Nothing is truly yours alone. That's why Jesus wants you to share what you have. When you share what Jesus has given you, then many people can enjoy it, instead of just you.

Your Turn

1. Why were the children fighting?
2. What should the children have done with the guitar?
3. When was the last time you shared something?

_____

_____

_____

_____

_____

Prayer

Dear Jesus, thank You for all of the things You have given me. Help me to share my blessings with others. Amen.

Tambourine Music

Read this to your child: "The children should have shared their guitar — that's what Jesus would want them to do. They also could have worked together to make more toys, which is something you could do, too. Even if you don't have a toy guitar, you can still have fun with a musical instrument. Just make your own. Remember to share it!"

You Will Need
- 2 aluminum pie plates
- beans, beads or buttons
- non-toxic glue or tape
- construction paper
- safety scissors
- crayons

What to Do
Help your child place some beans, beads, buttons or another small, hard item in a pie plate and then secure another plate, face-to-face, to it with glue or tape. Allow her to decorate her tambourine any way she likes.

 # Mercy

You should be merciful.
I desire mercy.
~Matthew 12:7

No TV Today

When Jillian forgot to clean up her room, she knew she would have to face the consequences. It was Saturday morning, and she and her big brother Kyle always watched cartoons. As Jillian sat down beside Kyle she heard Mom say, "No, Jillian. You didn't do your work, so you can't watch TV this morning."

"But I'm sorry, Mom, I'm sorry," Jillian cried. "Please, please let me watch TV."

Kyle, hearing his sister crying, wanted to help. "Just give her one more chance, Mom" he said. "Please. She just forgot."

Kyle felt sympathy for his sister. He knew that she hadn't cleaned her room like she was supposed to, but because she had just forgotten, he still showed Jillian mercy. In the same way, even though you may sometimes make mistakes, Jesus shows you mercy, and expects that you will do the same for others.

Your Turn

1. Why didn't Jillian clean her room?
2. Why did Kyle want to give Jillian a second chance to do her work?
3. Can you remember a time when you showed someone mercy?

_____

_____

_____

_____

_____

_____

_____

Prayer

Jesus, please help me be merciful to others. Thank You for the mercy You show me every day. Amen.

TV Time

Read this to your child: "Jesus shows mercy when you do wrong. He forgives your sins. Just like Kyle, you should show mercy to others when they are sorry for their mistakes. Color the picture of the television."

What is your favorite TV show?

_____

Comfort

Jesus is always with you to comfort you when you are hurt.
Cast all your anxiety on him because he cares for you.

~1 Peter 5:7

Comforting Arms

Melissa was having a great time. Daddy had set the tent up in the middle of the living room and she and her sisters had been "camping" for days. As Melissa pulled back the flaps and stepped through the opening, her foot caught on the bottom edge and she tripped. Falling forward, she hit her head on a table, leaving a deep cut above her left eye. The cut bled and Melissa cried. Not only did it hurt a lot, but tomorrow was her very first day of school and she didn't want to have a big bandage over her eye.

Daddy put some medicine and a bandage on Melissa's cut and then gave her a big hug. Melissa was still crying, but Daddy held her tight and told her that she would be all right. Feeling Daddy's strong arms around her made Melissa feel safe. The cut didn't seem so bad now that Daddy was there with her, whispering words of comfort in her ear.

Just like Melissa's daddy gave her comfort, Jesus comforts you. Jesus is always with you, even though you don't see Him. When you're sad or hurt, you can imagine Jesus' arms around you, holding you just like Melissa's daddy held her.

Your Turn

1. Why was Melissa crying?
2. What made Melissa feel better?
3. Can you think of some ways that you could comfort people who are sad?

_____

_____

_____

_____

_____

Prayer

Jesus, thank You for always being with me to guide me, and comfort me when I'm sad. Help me to comfort others as well. Amen.

Face Find

Read this to your child: "Melissa's feelings changed when Daddy comforted her. Jesus' love is like that, too. When you are sad or hurt, just think of Jesus and you are sure to feel a little better."

Draw a circle around the picture of how Melissa felt when she hit her head.

How did Melissa feel after her daddy hugged and comforted her?

Answer is on page 235.

Competition

Competition is good, as long as you play fairly.
Run in such a way as to get the prize.
~1 Corinthians 9:24

Winning Isn't Everything

"He shoots, he scores!" yelled Kenny as he threw his arms high in the air, happy he had won. Jackie chased after the ball again. Even though she was two years younger than her big brother, she tried very hard to beat Kenny, but Kenny was so much bigger that he easily scored another goal in a matter of seconds. Jackie tried again and again, but Kenny was just too big. No matter how hard she tried, Jackie was too little to score a goal against her big brother.

Kenny was so happy that he was winning the game that he didn't seem to notice how bad Jackie felt about losing. Each time he scored another goal against her, Jackie looked as if she would cry. She eventually gave up and walked away with a very sad look on her face.

It is good to be competitive. Jesus wants you to do your very best, but not if it means hurting others. Kenny wasn't playing fairly with Jackie. She was too little to beat Kenny, and didn't even have a chance of winning. All he cared about was scoring points and winning the game. You should try to improve yourself every day, and remember that doing your best is more important than "winning."

Your Turn

1. Why wasn't Jackie able to score a goal against her big brother?
2. Do you think Jackie and Kenny's game was fair?
3. Is it good or bad to be competitive?

_____

_____

_____

_____

_____

_____

Prayer

Jesus, please help me to remember that winning isn't everything. Amen.

Tiny Hoops

Read this to your child: "Playing games is fun. Winning is even more fun, but not if you hurt someone at the same time. Jesus wants you to be competitive and do your best to win at games, but He also wants you to play fair. Here is a new game to play:"

Use this outline to trace the basketball hoop onto a piece of cardboard. Cut the outline out of the cardboard and fold it on the dashed lines. Set something on the base to steady it. Cut out the center of the hoop, and you're ready to play. Any small wadded-up piece of paper will do nicely for a ball.

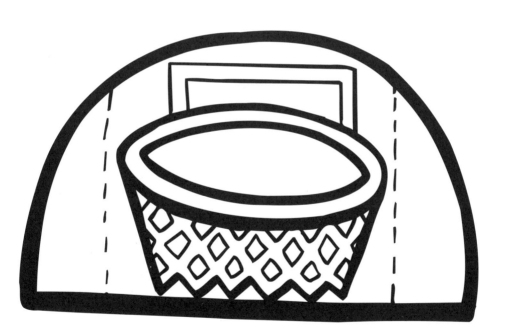

Compromise

Working together makes us all stronger.
Two are better than one.
~Ecclesiastes 4:9

Building Castles Together

Lindsey was trying her best to build a castle with wooden blocks. One by one she stacked the blocks on top of each other. Once she even had all four walls of the castle almost done when they went crashing to the floor. Lindsey tried and tried, but no matter how hard she worked at it, the blocks kept falling down before she could finish.

"Patrick," she called upstairs to her brother, "can you come down and help me build my castle?" Lindsey was very good at deciding how the castle should look, but Patrick was better at knowing which blocks should go where to make the castle walls strong.

A few minutes later Patrick came downstairs and together he and Lindsey built a giant castle with doors, windows and even a flag for the top.

You are stronger when you cooperate with others, because each of us is good at different things. When people work together, we all bring our special skills to a project, which is why we can then do so much more.

Lindsey and Patrick knew that if they built the castle together, it would be much better. Jesus wants you to be that way with your life. He wants you to work with others and help them, using the special skills that He gave you to make the world a better place.

Your Turn

1. Why did Lindsey ask Patrick to help her?
2. Why is cooperation a good thing?
3. What are some ways that you cooperate with others?

_____

_____

_____

_____

_____

Prayer

Thank You, Jesus, for giving me special skills that I can help others with. Please help me to cooperate with others whenever I can. Amen.

Make Your Own Blocks!

Read this to your child: "Jesus wants you to work together, using all of the special abilities He has given to help others. This project is perfect for doing with someone else."

What You Need
- white paper
- construction paper
- tape
- crayons
- scissors

What to Do
1. Trace the pattern onto white paper.
2. Allow your child to decorate the box with crayons.
3. Cut out the box on the solid lines.
4. Have your child help you fold the box on the dashed lines.
5. Tape to secure the box.

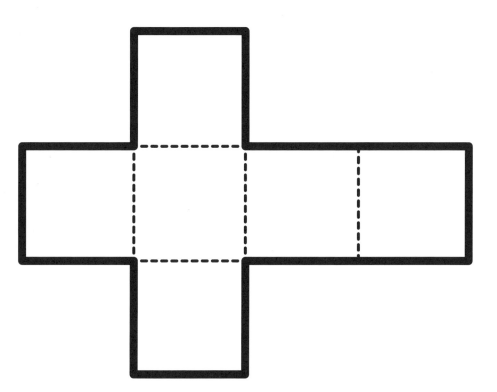

Teasing

Teasing is only okay if it doesn't hurt anyone.
He will yet fill your mouth with laughter.

~Job 8:21

You Squished It!

Amy and Mom were driving to the shopping mall when, all of a sudden, a big brown, fuzzy squirrel darted out into the road. Mom swerved to the side of the road to miss the squirrel, squealing the tires as she did. Luckily, the squirrel made it safely to the other side.

"We missed it, Amy," Mom said. But Amy responded, "You squished it!"

"No, I didn't," Mom insisted. "The squirrel is OK."

"You mashed it!" said Amy giggling.

"Amy," said Mom, a bit annoyed now, "I didn't hit the squirrel."

Amy looked at Mom, her eyes sparkling with mischief, and said, "The squirrel went SPLAT!"

Now even Mom couldn't help but laugh, too, and she and Amy both giggled the rest of the way to the mall.

Sometimes teasing can be hurtful to people, like when a playground bully says things that are mean to you. But teasing can also be fun. Amy knew how to tease her Mom in a fun way that doesn't hurt anyone, and that's wonderful! Jesus wants you to love and care for others. Sometimes teasing can be a way to show your love and make someone happy.

Your Turn

1. Why did Amy tease her mom?
2. Was Amy teasing her mom in a fun way, or a bad, hurtful way?
3. Can you remember when you last teased someone? Did you do it in a good or bad way?

_____

_____

_____

_____

_____

Prayer

Dear Jesus, I know that teasing can be a lot of fun. Help me to only tease in a way that is fun for everyone, and never hurtful or mean. Amen.

Make Squirrel/Bird Feeders

Read this to your child: "Jesus wants us to be happy and make others happy, too. There are many fun ways to do that. Amy loves wildlife, even if she is teasing about it. Here are some fun things she likes to do to help her animal friends."

What You Need
• string or yarn
• cookie cutters
• bread
• O-shaped cereal
• peanut butter
• birdseed
• pine cones

What to Do
1. Cut the bread into small shapes. Stale or thick bread works best.
2. Leave the bread plain or help your child to coat the bread with a thin layer of peanut butter and roll in birdseed.
3. Thread string through the center.
4. Have your child help you hang the mini-feeder in a tree.

Other Ideas:
Show your child how to thread cereal with string, and hang it outside.
Roll a pine cone in peanut butter, then bird seed, and hang.

Possessiveness

God wants you to share what He has given you.
Be devoted to one another in brotherly love.

~Romans 12:10

Mine!

"She's my baby!" yelled Holly at Evan.

"No, Holly," answered Evan. "She's everybody's baby."

"No, no she's not! She's mine!" Holly yelled even louder.

"Holly," Evan explained, "Baby Tina is my sister, too, so she's your baby and my baby, and Sarah's baby, and Mom and Daddy's baby."

"No!" screamed Holly at the top of her lungs as she grabbed Tina in her walker and wheeled her from the room. Holly took Tina into the bedroom and closed the door, but Tina didn't want to be in the bedroom. Tina wanted to play with all of the kids. She started to cry.

Holly loved her baby sister Tina so much that she didn't want to share her. She wanted baby Tina to be hers and hers alone. If Holly really loved Tina, however, she should have shared her with her brother and sisters. By being selfish and possessive, neither she nor Tina had any fun. If they had played together, they all would have had fun.

Jesus doesn't want you to be possessive of people or things. Everything you have is a gift from God, so nothing really belongs to you anyway.

Your Turn

1. What did Holly do that was wrong?
2. Did Holly's possessiveness make baby Tina happy?
3. Can you think of something or someone whom you have acted possessive of?

_____

_____

_____

_____

_____

_____

Prayer

Jesus, please help me to remember that everything I have is a gift from You. Amen.

I Can Share

Read this to your child: "Everything you have is a gift from God. He wants you to share all of His gifts. Here are some things that you can share with others. Color them, and then circle the one that is your favorite thing to share. Whom do you like to share with?"

Criticism

You should look for the good in people.
Do not judge, or you too will be judged.
~Matthew 7:1

Understanding Rudeness

The grocery story cashier wasn't very friendly at all. Julie said hi to him, but the cashier didn't answer. Julie asked him if she could help, but the cashier said no without even looking up. Most people would have given up trying to talk to such a rude person, but Julie continued. By the time the cashier had finished adding up all the items in Mom's grocery cart, Julie had spoken to the man several more times, but received little or no answer. As they left the store, Mom said to Julie, "That guy wasn't very nice was he?"

Julie paused a moment and then said, "He was nice."

"Did you say 'nice'?" Mom asked, thinking she must have heard her wrong. Julie nodded.

"How can you say he was nice?" Mom asked, surprised by Julie's response. "I thought he was rude."

"Hey look, Mom, maybe he was just having a bad day. He wasn't that bad," Julie said.

We are all sinners, and just like Julie, we should look for the good in people instead of thinking only about the bad. Jesus made you special. If you look deep enough, you can find something good in all people, even those who behave badly.

Your Turn

1. Why did Julie's mother think the cashier was rude?
2. What did Julie think of the cashier?
3. Can you think of some other reasons to explain why the cashier behaved so rudely?

_____

_____

_____

_____

_____

_____

Prayer

Jesus, please help me to always look for the best in people. Amen.

Grocery Puzzle

Read this to your child: "Julie was able to look for the special part of the cashier that Jesus made in all of us. If you look beyond the bad things people do, you can also find the good in people. Here is one of Julie's favorite things to buy at the grocery store. We made a puzzle out of our drawing, and you can do the same. Just draw one of your favorite grocery items on a piece of paper and then have your mom or dad cut it into pieces for you—then you have your very own puzzle! If you like milk, you can trace this puzzle and cut it out."

Encouragement

Jesus encourages you to always do your best.
Look to the Lord and his strength.
~1 Chronicles 16:11

You can do it!

"Come on, Perry, you can do it," called Sue to her big brother.

"No, Sue," Perry said. "I don't want to." Sue and Perry were outside on their new bikes teaching themselves to ride, while Daddy watched from where he was working in the garage.

"Do it, Perry" Sue insisted. "You can do it." Perry looked scared, but his sister's encouragement gave him the courage to try. Taking a firm hold of the handlebars, and carefully swinging his leg over to sit on the seat, Perry slowly pushed off and began to peddle. He made it a short distance, but was moving too slowly so the bike soon tipped over.

"Go faster, Perry," Daddy called after him. Perry pushed off again and started peddling, but each time the bike tipped and he had to start over again. Perry tried again, and again and again. Sue kept calling out to him to keep trying, and eventually he was able to ride down the driveway without tipping over.

Sue's encouragement gave Perry the courage to try something that he was afraid to do. In the same way, Jesus encourages you every day to try new things and do your best. The words He gives us in the Bible tell us how we should live our lives, but also encourage us by Jesus' great love for us.

Your Turn

1. Why was Perry scared to ride his new bike?
2. How did Sue help Perry ride his bike?
3. Can you think of a time when you helped someone by encouraging him or her?

Prayer

Thank You, Jesus, for all of Your encouragement, and for loving me so much. Please help me to also encourage others whenever I can. Amen.

What to Ride

Read this to your child: "Sue encouraged Perry just like Jesus encourages you every day. If you read the Bible, Jesus' words will show you the way to do your very best. Now let the dots show you the way to draw this picture, and you can color it."

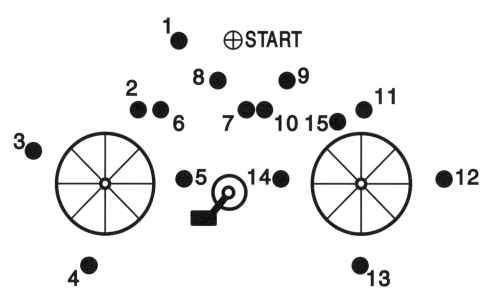

Answer is on page 235.

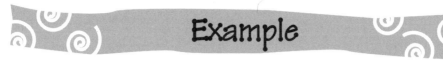

Example

We should set a good example for others.
Set them an example by doing what is good.

~Titus 2:7

Why Do I Have to Be an Example?

"Get down off the table," Mom ordered. Shandra had climbed up onto the top of the toy picnic table. "You're setting a bad example for your sisters," she added.

Shandra sadly climbed down but started to complain. "Why do I have to be an example?" she asked.

"We're all examples," explained Mom. "When people see someone else do something, they can get the idea that they should do it, too. That's why we need to always behave ourselves."

Later that same day, Shandra learned how important it is to set a good example for others. While Shandra was watching TV, little Mollie climbed to the top of the picnic table just like Shandra had. Because she was so much younger than Shandra, she almost fell off. "Do you see what can happen when you set a bad example, Shandra?" asked Mom. "Mollie could have hurt herself very badly if she had fallen, and she never would have even thought about climbing up there if she hadn't seen you do it first."

Shandra learned an important lesson that day. She learned that we must set a good example, but not just for brothers and sisters. We need to set a good example for everyone. As a Christian, you need to show the world what it means to live like Jesus taught. Jesus says to teach others about Him whenever you can. The best way you can do that is by living a godly life and setting a good example for others.

Your Turn

1. Why was Shandra upset with what Mom told her?
2. What almost happened to Mollie as a result of Shandra's setting a bad example?
3. Do you ever set a bad example for others?

_____

_____

_____

Prayer

Jesus, I want to set a good example for others. Please help me to always behave in a way that would make You proud of me. Amen.

Good Example, Bad Example

Read this to your child: "The best way to show how much you love Jesus is by doing what the Bible tells you to do. By setting a 'good example,' you show the world what it means to be a Christian. Color the picture that shows the girl setting a good example for others. Draw an X through the pictures where she is setting a bad example."

Answer is on page 235.

Friendship

There is more to friendship than just having fun.
A friend loves at all times.
~Proverbs 17:17

Being a Friend

Matthew and Leanna's friend Kelsey had been in a terrible accident. She had been hurt very badly and now she was in the hospital. They felt sad for Kelsey, and wanted to do everything they could to make her feel better.

While Kelsey was in the hospital, and even after she came home, Matthew and Leanna did their best to make her happy by sending her special things that they made themselves. Matthew painted pictures with bright colors and made fun mazes for Kelsey to play with. Leanna did her part too by drawing pretty pictures of animals and houses to send. Both Matthew and Leanna never forgot that their friend needed them, and even months following Kelsey's accident they asked about her.

Eventually Kelsey was feeling better again, but it took a long time.

Matthew and Leanna knew the importance of friendship, and the responsibility that goes along with having a friend. Friends aren't just for doing fun things. Friends are there to help when you need them, and need help themselves sometimes, too. Jesus teaches to care for others more than you care for yourself, and the love and caring that you share with friends is a good example of this.

Your Turn

1. Why did Kelsey need extra caring from her friends?
2. What did Matthew and Leanna do to care for their friend?
3. How do you show your friends that you care about them?

_____

_____

_____

_____

_____

Prayer

Dear Jesus, I want to be a good friend. Please help me to know when my friends need me, and how to show them I care. Amen.

Love Notes

Read this to your child: "Jesus wants you to love others more than yourself. He wants you to show them that you love them. These Love Notes are a great way to do that."

What You Need
• construction paper
• any combination of the following:
    non-toxic markers
    glitter
    non-toxic glue

What to Do
Fold construction paper in fourths, like a card, for your child. Show how to use the materials you provide to make a special greeting card. Tell your child that the card should be for someone she loves—not for any special holiday, but just because she loves him or her.

Humility

You should be humble.
Be completely humble and gentle.

~Ephesians 4:2

Robbie's Bragging

"I win. I win," bragged Robbie as he threw his arms up into the air in happiness. "I always win 'cause I'm the best," he continued. Robbie had just won another video game, and he was ready to play again...but he couldn't find anyone to play with.

"Come on, Sheila" Robbie said to his sister. "Come and play a game with me." Sheila just looked at Robbie and shook her head.

"Sheila, please come and play with me. C'mon, it'll be fun," Robbie said.

Still, Sheila just shook her head no. "Mom, Sheila won't play with me," said Robbie. "Make her play with me!"

"Maybe," Mom responded, "Sheila won't play with you because you brag too much. If you acted like that when I played with you, I wouldn't want to play with you anymore either."

Bragging is not a nice or polite thing to do. It isn't how Jesus wants you to behave either. Jesus teaches that humility is a far better thing to show others. It's okay to be proud of your accomplishments, but you shouldn't brag or be boastful to others.

Your Turn

1. What did Robbie do that was wrong?
2. Why didn't Sheila want to play with Robbie anymore?
3. How should Robbie have behaved with his sister?

_____

_____

_____

_____

_____

_____

Prayer

Jesus, sometimes it can be easy to brag about things I've done. Please help me to remember that being humble makes You happy. Amen.

Where's the Game

Read this to your child: "Jesus wants you to do the best you can, but He doesn't want you to brag. Bragging makes other people feel badly, which is something Robbie has to learn. Connect the dots to see one of Robbie's favorite things to play video games on. Can you guess what it is before you connect the dots?"

Answer is on page 236.

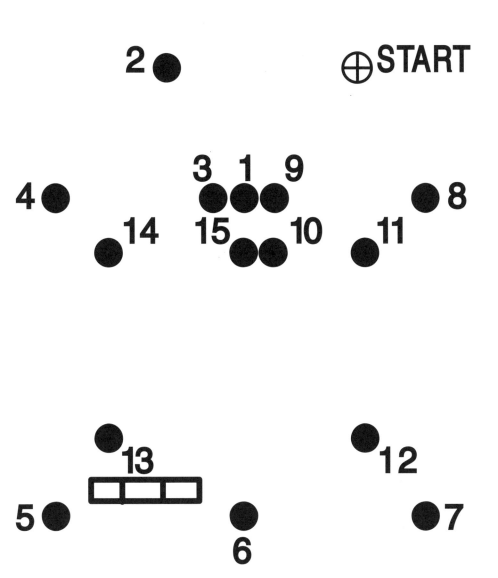

Insults

You should not call people hurtful names.
Do to others what you would have them do to you.
~Matthew 7:12

Name Calling

"Cody! You boarhead!" yelled Bessie at her big brother, Cody, as he ran into the house. Every day she met Cody's bus at the road when he came home from kindergarten, and every day he stepped on the anthills in the driveway as they walked in. Bessie liked to play with the anthills. Cody liked to tease her by stepping on them.

"Bessie," said Mom as they entered the house, "it's not nice to call Cody names."

Bessie scowled and said, "Cody's a pig!"

Mom stopped Bessie, looked at her and said, "You wouldn't like Cody to call you names, so don't call him names."

Bessie thought about what Mom said. She didn't call Cody any more names...at least for the rest of the day.

Jesus doesn't like when you call people hurtful names. When you call someone a bad name it can hurt that person's feelings. You shouldn't hurt other people. Jesus taught to treat people the same way you want to be treated. So, if you ever want to call someone a name, stop and think first how you'd feel if someone said that to you.

Your Turn

1. Why did Bessie call Cody a bad name?
2. Is it wrong to call people hurtful names? Why?
3. How would you feel if someone called you a bad name?

_____

_____

_____

_____

_____

Prayer

Help me, Jesus, to treat people the way I would like to be treated and never hurt anyone. Amen.

Crawling Count

Read this to your child: "Jesus taught to treat others the same way you want to be treated. If Cody were behaving the way Jesus wants him to, he would never have stepped on Bessie's anthills. Here's a picture of an anthill, just like the ones Bessie loves so much. Can you count how many ants are on the hill?"

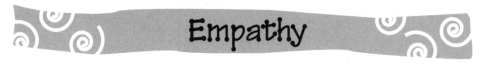

Empathy

You should try to understand how other people feel.
Cry aloud for understanding.

~Proverbs 2:3

Understanding Other People's Feelings

Beverly was happily watching one of her favorite cartoons when suddenly the characters in the show lost their little dog. They searched far and wide but couldn't find him. The children on the show cried and cried because they were so sad that they had lost their dog.

Beverly felt so sad about the lost little dog that she started to cry, too. Soon Beverly was crying so hard that even Mom and big brother Joseph couldn't calm her down.

Mom tried hugging Beverly very tightly, but that didn't help. Joseph sang a song and danced in front of Beverly, but Beverly just cried harder. When nothing else worked, Mom decided to make Beverly watch the rest of the TV show. When Beverly saw that the children on the show found their little dog in the end, she finally stopped crying.

Beverly's crying is a good example of "empathy." Empathy is when you feel what other people are feeling. Beverly felt sad just like the children in the TV show felt sad. She felt so much like they did in fact, that she cried just like they were crying. In the same way, Beverly only felt happy again when the kids in the show felt happy, too.

It's a good thing to feel "empathy" for others. Empathy helps you to understand how other people think and feel, and why they do the things they do. When you understand other people it is easier for you to see the good in them, and love them just as Jesus loves and understands you.

Your Turn

1. Why was little Beverly crying?
2. Was it good or bad that Beverly understood how the kids in the TV show felt?
3. Do you remember a time when you felt sad just because someone else was feeling sad?

_____

_____

Prayer

Jesus, thank You for giving me the ability to feel how other people are feeling. Please help me do my best to understand others, and why they do the things that they do. Amen.

Happy Girl/Sad Girl

Read this to your child: "Jesus wants you to have empathy for others so you can better understand and help people. How much empathy do you have? Match each picture with how you think that person is feeling."

Answer is on page 236.

Accidents

You must trust Jesus to know what is best for you.
Call out for insight and cry aloud for understanding.
~Proverbs 2:3

Why Do Accidents Happen?

"Did you ever see a really bad car accident, Mom?" asked Martha. She had become very interested lately in why car accidents happen.

"I didn't see it happen," answered Mom, "but Grandpa was in a pretty bad accident several years ago."

"Can you tell me about it?" asked Martha, anxious to hear the details.

Mom began telling Martha how while the police were chasing a bad man through the streets of town, the bad man's truck ran into the back of Grandpa's car. Grandpa was hurt very badly, and it was a long time before he was okay.

Martha listened very carefully to the story. When it was over, she asked question after question about the accident.

Accidents happen. Some are very scary, like when someone is hurt in a car accident, or when someone gets very sick. Other bad things that happen are less frightening, like when you spill a cup of milk. No matter what type of accident you see, however, they all can be hard to understand.

Martha wants to understand why car "accidents" happen. By asking about her grandpa's accident, Martha is trying to learn how and why it happened. In the same way, it's good for you to ask lots of questions about Jesus. It helps you to understand His plan for you. You may never completely understand why Jesus allows accidents, but if you understand that Jesus controls everything that happens, you don't really have to know "why." You can just trust Him to know what's best.

Your Turn

1. Why did Martha want to know about car accidents?
2. Can anyone always know why accidents happen?
3. Why is it good to ask lots of questions?

_____

_____

_____

_____

Prayer

Thank You, Jesus, for taking care of us all. Help me to trust You even when I don't understand why You let some things happen. Amen.

Accident Answers

Read this to your child: "Jesus causes all things to happen for your own good, but He still wants you to be careful and avoid some accidents when you can. Look at the following examples of some accidents. How could each have been avoided? When you're done thinking it over, color the pictures."

Parenting

Like Jesus, parents are here to love you and take care of you.
[Nothing] will be able to separate us from the love of God.

~Romans 8:39

Building Nests

"Let's build a nest," said Adelle to Erin. One by one, Erin dragged blankets, rugs and pillows to the center of the living room, where Adelle carefully placed them in a circle around baby Grace. It took a long time, but they finally were able to build a large nest and Adelle took good care of it.

Each time Erin caught one of the blankets with her foot, or baby Grace pushed a pillow outside the nest, Adelle quickly replaced it. If Grace crawled over the side, Adelle carefully placed the baby safely back inside the middle of the nest. Sometimes Adelle forgot for a moment or two. A cartoon would come on TV or little Erin would want to play chase, but Adelle still kept careful watch over her precious nest. She was a good little "mother."

Being a parent is one of the greatest blessings God can give, but it's also a lot of work. Like Adelle with her nest, your parents have to take good care of the home they've make for you, and watch over you very closely.

Jesus is like a parent to everyone. He watches over you, loves you, and is never distracted by other things. As with your parents, you can count on Jesus to take care of you.

Your Turn

1. Why was Adelle a good "little mother"?
2. What do parents do to take care of their children?
3. How is Jesus like a parent?

_____

_____

_____

_____

_____

_____

_____

Prayer

Thank You, Jesus, for giving me parents, and thank You also for being like a parent to all of us. Amen.

Busy Parents

Read this to your child: "Jesus is like a parent to everyone, even grown-ups. He gives everyone the blessing of a mom and dad to take care of kids as well. Circle the things that parents do, then color the pictures."

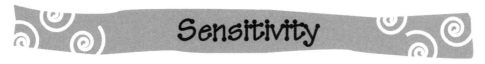

Sensitivity

Sensitivity helps you understand and help others.
Encourage the timid, help the weak, be patient with everyone.
~1 Thessalonians 5:14

Scary School Bus

The bus was finally coming. They could see the shining headlights far down the road. As it drew nearer, the bright yellow paint of the school bus came into view, causing a cheer of excitement from both Donna and Lily, who had been waiting patiently for it. They knew that soon the bus would stop and their big brother Louis would be home from kindergarten to play with them.

"Here it comes," said Donna.

"Bus, bus," screamed Lily, jumping up and down. Lily was happy to see the school bus coming toward her, but as it pulled up, she started to worry. The bus didn't look so large when it was far down the road. Now that it was right in front of her, it was very, very big.

"No, no, no," screamed Lily suddenly as she wildly shook her head back and forth. The bus that seemed so wonderful a moment ago was now just big, loud and scary. Tears rolled down her cheeks and she shook with fear.

Donna loved few things more than greeting Louis as he stepped off the bus, but as she heard Lily's screams, she couldn't ignore her little sister's need. Turning away from the bus, Donna ran to her sister's side instead. As soon as she put her arms around little Lily, Lily stopped screaming.

Donna's sensitivity to her sister's feelings gave her an understanding of what Lily needed. Hopefully you can be sensitive to the needs and feelings of others. As with this story, if you are sensitive to others, you are better able to help them, and Jesus certainly wants you to help other people as much as you can.

Your Turn

1. Why was Lily so scared?
2. How did Donna help her little sister?
3. Can you remember a time when being sensitive helped you understand how to help someone?

_____

_____

Prayer

Please help me, Jesus, to be sensitive to the needs and feelings of others, so that I can help other people. Amen.

Track the Bus

Read this to your child: "Jesus wants you to help others. The best way to do that is by being sensitive to their needs. Today Louis's school bus could use some help. Can you guide his school bus to his house?"

Answer is on page 236.

Charity

You should help others.
Whoever sows generously will also reap generously.

~2 Corinthians 9:6

Cheryl's Charity

"Stop it, Maggie," said Cheryl as she picked up the stuffed animals and teething rings. Baby Maggie had dropped her toys off her walker tray for the third time, and now she couldn't reach them again.

With a deep sigh, Cheryl put the toys on the tray again. "There you go, Maggie" said Cheryl. "Now don't drop them again." Cheryl returned to the drawing she was working on, but moments later, Maggie once again knocked her toys onto the floor. Again, Cheryl picked up the toys. No matter how many times Maggie dropped them, Cheryl helped her.

Why did Cheryl take care of Maggie? By helping Maggie, did Cheryl get a present, money or prizes? No. There was no visible reward for Cheryl helping Maggie.

She did it simply because it needed to be done. Maggie wasn't able to take care of herself, and so Cheryl, who was older, helped her.

Charity is like that. Jesus gave you a body, mind and many special abilities. When you see someone who doesn't have the same blessings as you and needs your help, Jesus wants you to do what you can to make things better for that person. He gave Himself on the cross to save us from our sins. If Jesus could do all that for us, shouldn't we do as much as we can for each other?

Your Turn

1. How did Cheryl help baby Maggie?
2. Why should you help other people?
3. When have you helped someone?

_____

_____

_____

_____

_____

Prayer

Thank You, Jesus, for dying for my sins. Please help me to always show charity to others, even when it's hard to do. Amen.

Drum to Make

Read this to your child: "Cheryl took good care of Maggie because she knew that Jesus would want her to. She loves Maggie just as Jesus loves her. One of baby Maggie's favorite toys is a toy drum (or anything else she can bang on). You can easily make a drum of your own with some things from around the house."

What You Need
- empty container
- masking tape
- construction paper
- non-toxic glue
- crayons and markers
- glitter
- glue-on decorations

What to Do
1. Empty oatmeal, whipped cream or butter containers work well for this project. Just clean the container well and use some masking tape to secure the top if necessary.
2. Give the container to your child to decorate. We like to wrap an oatmeal container in construction paper that we have colored with pretty pictures. Then we add some glitter to make it sparkle. Note: if you place some buttons (or other small items) into the container before sealing it, you can also shake your drum to make "music."

God Made Me Smart

Problem Solving

I can figure out things if I just think about them long enough.
Make every effort to add to your faith...knowledge.

~2 Peter 1:5

How Does Santa Do That?

Janie was listening to a story about Santa Claus. She loved the story, and listened very carefully as her mom read it to her while they snuggled together on the living room couch. She heard how Santa brings presents to all of the little children of the world, how he travels through the night on Christmas Eve in his sled and how he slides down chimneys to get into houses.

After patiently listening to the story about Santa, Janie sat quietly on the couch, staring at the thin fireplace chimney in the living room. She was confused about something. Janie wondered how Santa could fit down the chimney. After a few minutes, Janie said, "Santa must be skinny!"

Even when you're confused about something, you can often understand it if you think about it long enough. Janie couldn't understand how Santa Claus could get down the narrow chimney in her house. After thinking it over, Janie was able to come up with a reason. Just like Janie, you can solve problems and figure out how to do new things if you just work at it. God likes when you use your brain, because He created it.

Your Turn

1. What did Janie have a hard time figuring out?
2. How did Janie finally decide Santa was able to get down the chimney?
3. Why should we think about things that we don't understand?

_____

_____

_____

_____

_____

Prayer

Thank You, Jesus, for helping me think things through so I can figure out how things work. Please help me to never give up trying to understand new things. Amen.

Figure It Out

Read this to your child: "One of the best gifts Jesus gave you is a brain to think about things. Using your brain, you can figure out stuff just like Janie did. Janie managed to come up with an explanation for how Santa gets into her house. Now can you find your way to her Christmas tree?"

Answer is on page 236.

Loss

God teaches that loss isn't permanent.
So do not fear, for I am with you.
~Isaiah 41:10

Where's Daddy?

Wendy was so excited when she woke up! All week long her daddy had been home on vacation, and she couldn't wait to run into the bedroom and kiss him good morning.

Wendy ran to her daddy's bedroom and peeked over the side of his bed. No Daddy. She ran to the other side of the bed and slowly peeked over the bunched up comforter, but still no Daddy. Wendy was scared now. She clutched the bed-covers and struggled to pull herself up onto the bed. Standing in the middle of the bed, she could see that Daddy was gone. With tears flowing down her cheeks, Wendy closed her eyes and screamed, "Daddy!"

The entire day Wendy cried and called "Daddy." It wasn't until her daddy returned home from work that Wendy stopped crying. When Wendy saw Daddy, she was so happy to see him that she gave him a big hug and a kiss.

Have you ever worried that someone you love wasn't coming back? Jesus wants you to know that He will never leave you, that he is always by your side and that we will all be with Him someday in Heaven.

Your Turn

1. What do you think Wendy was thinking while she was looking for her daddy?
2. Have you ever worried that your mommy or daddy was gone?
3. When you're worried about your parents being gone, what makes you feel better?

_____

_____

_____

_____

_____

Prayer

Thank You, Jesus, for Your promise to never leave me. Amen.

Where Are You?

Just as a game of peek-a-boo can teach object permanence to an infant, a game of hide and seek is a fun way to demonstrate to a preschooler that our loved ones are still with us even though we don't always see them. Have your child stand facing a corner while you quickly hide, then call her name and enjoy listening to her mirthful giggles as she looks for you. After your game is over, remind your child that, just as in your game of peek-a-boo, even though she cannot "see" Jesus, He is always with her. If you don't have time to play hide and seek right now, here's a picture of Wendy looking for her daddy that you and your child can color together.

 # Listening

We need to listen carefully to people, and to Jesus' teachings.
Everyone should be quick to listen.

~James 1:19

Listen to Me!

The earrings were the prettiest Victoria had ever seen. They were tiny pink stones, perfectly round, with a shiny gold setting around them. How they sparkled in the lights as they sat on the store shelf! Victoria wanted them so much—much more than she had wanted anything all day, but Mom said the earrings were only for little girls who had pierced ears, which Victoria didn't.

Mom and Victoria continued shopping, and Victoria kept asking Mom if she could have the earrings. Finally Mom stopped and scolded Victoria. Then taking Victoria by the shoulders, Mom looked her straight in the eye and asked, "Victoria, what did I say?"

Victoria immediately said, "Can I have those pretty earrings, please, please, please?"

"Now, Victoria," said Mom again, "you've already asked me that question many times, and I've already answered you. I want you to think now—what was my answer?"

Victoria was very still and quiet for a moment, then answered, "You said no...but I want it, I want it!"

"Victoria, you have your answer," said Mom. "If you'd been paying attention in the first place, you wouldn't have been scolded for not listening to me."

Just like Victoria, sometimes you may need to slow down and pay attention or you miss what's being said to you. It's important to listen carefully to what your parents tell you because they know what's best.

For the same reason, it's also important to listen to what Jesus tells you. Sometimes you may get too excited about what you want, and forget that it's what Jesus wants for you that's more important. He knows what's best for you.

Your Turn

1. What did Victoria want at the store?
2. Why did Victoria get scolded?
3. Why is it so important to listen carefully to what's said to you?

Prayer

Thank You, Jesus, for teaching me what's best. Please help me to listen. Amen.

Listen and Learn

Read this to your child: "Listening to your parents and to what the Bible teaches is very important. Jesus wants you to listen well because He wants you to be healthy and happy and have a good life. Here are pictures of times when you may not listen well. Do you always listen well in these situations?" Discuss these with your child, then have her color the pictures.

Patience

If you want something, don't give up. Keep trying.
If we hope for what we do not yet have,
we wait for it patiently.

~Romans 8:25

Patience Pays Off

Maddie stared at the white cardboard card in front of her. The letter "A" stared back at her as she tried to tell her Mom the name of the letter she was seeing. After a few moments of thought, it came to her. "A," she said, "It's the letter A."

"Very good" said Mom, "I'm so proud of you."

Maddie couldn't wait until she learned all of her ABCs. Mom had told her that when Maddie could tell her the names of every letter on the flash cards she showed her she would get a special prize. Every day Maddie practiced the alphabet, but some days it was really hard to do. Sometimes she thought she'd rather watch TV or ride her bike when it came time to practice.

For several weeks Maddie practiced her ABCs, but every time Mom showed her the flash cards she would make at least one or two mistakes. One day Aunt Kathy came to visit to watch her do her alphabet. When Mom brought out the flash cards, Maddie didn't make any mistakes. She got every single one of the flash cards correct. All of her hard work and patience had finally paid off. She knew her ABCs!

Mom was so proud of her that Maddie got three special prizes — a doll, doll clothes and some barrettes. Maddie had earned her prizes. Jesus gave you the ability to learn, but it doesn't always happen easily. Jesus wants you to work very hard to learn new things so you can work for Him.

Your Turn

1. Why did Maddie want to learn her ABCs?
2. Why was it hard sometimes for Maddie to practice her alphabet?
3. Do you remember a time when it took you a long time to learn something?

_____

_____

_____

_____

Prayer

Please give me patience Jesus, to do all the things I need to do. Amen.

The First Letter

Read this to your child: "Circle the card that has the letter A on it. Remember, don't give up even if you are not sure which letter is the A. Jesus gave you the ability to learn. You should work hard to make the best use of the gift He has given you."

 # Learning

We should learn something every day.
Choose...knowledge rather than choice gold.

~Proverbs 8:10

Let's Bake a Cake

Brooke carefully set out all of her toy spoons and forks as she got things ready for the pretend meal that she and her little sister were making.

"We need another cup of flour," said Brooke as she and little Debbie played at their toy kitchen set.

"One, two, three," counted Brooke as Debbie dumped the pretend cups of flour into the kitchen sink. Brooke stirred in the sink with a tiny, yellow spoon as Debbie continued to dump more imaginary flour in.

"No," Brooke yelled suddenly. "You're putting too much in! Stop, stop." Debbie screamed and threw the whole cup in the sink.

"Debbie," scolded Brooke, "you're going to ruin the birthday cake! Now take some of that flour out." Debbie pretended to scoop the flour out of the sink, and they continued playing happily.

You learn every day. Even when you think you're just playing, you're learning, too. Brooke and Debbie thought they were just play-baking, but they were also learning how to count, add and follow directions.

Jesus wants you to keep learning more every day of your life. He even wants grown-ups to keep getting smarter and smarter so that they can be the best they can possibly be.

Your Turn

1. What were Brooke and Debbie pretending to do?
2. What kinds of things were Brooke and Debbie learning?
3. Can you think of something you've learned by playing?

_____

_____

_____

_____

_____

Prayer

Jesus, please help me get the most out of everything I do, even if I'm just playing. Amen.

Dough Ornaments

Read this to your child: "Jesus wants you to keep learning because He wants you to be the best Christian you can be. Learning new things helps you to be a better person. Here is something new for you to learn:"

What You Need

- 2 cups flour
- 1 cup water
- 1 cup salt
- 1/4 teaspoon cream of tartar
- non-staining food coloring or marking pens (optional)
- string or yarn

What to Do

Debbie and Brooke love to cook together. Here's one of their favorite recipes. They like it because when they're done "cooking," they have something pretty to hang up or play with. Mix the first four ingredients. Roll and cut out the dough just like you would make cookie cut-outs. Make a small hole for hanging the ornament later. Bake the "cookies" in a 225 degree oven for 2 to 3 hours (or until the centers harden as well as the outside edges). Cool completely. If you want a smooth finish you can use sandpaper to buff off the rough spots, or use food coloring and marking pens to decorate. Hang the ornament with string or yarn.

Boredom

I need to keep learning, even if it's boring sometimes.
Let us not become weary in doing good.

~Galatians 6:9

Adam Is Boring Me!

Adam and Cindy were watching a TV show about how tornadoes are made. Cindy didn't understand what they were watching. Adam decided to help her by explaining the TV show to her.

"Cindy, listen to me," Adam said as he tried to explain what they were watching. "There's stormy weather," he said, pointing to the screen. "Moist air condenses with hot air and the wind mixes together...and makes a tornado."

Cindy listened for a while as she watched the show about storms, but then started to fidget in her chair. She didn't understand what Adam was saying, and she was feeling tired, too. She wished they could just watch cartoons now and forget about learning about stormy weather. As Adam started to explain again how a tornado is made, she didn't want to listen anymore and hollered, "Mom, Adam's boring me!"

Cindy didn't want to keep learning important things, but Jesus wants you to be the best that you can be. He wants you to keep learning and to spend your time wisely. It's OK to feel bored sometimes, as long as you don't let it stop you from making good choices about how you spend your time.

Your Turn

1. Why didn't Cindy want to learn about storms?
2. Why does Jesus want you to use your time wisely?
3. Have you ever been bored?

_____

_____

_____

_____

_____

Prayer

Jesus, please help me to keep learning, even if I get bored, so I can keep growing stronger and smarter every day. Amen.

The Cross

Read this to your child: "One thing that should never bore you is your faith in Jesus. A common way to show that faith is by wearing the symbol of the cross. The cross is an important symbol of your faith in Jesus. It reminds you how important Jesus is to you and that you need to live the way He wants you to. Color only the squares with the number 1 in them, and you'll see the cross appear."

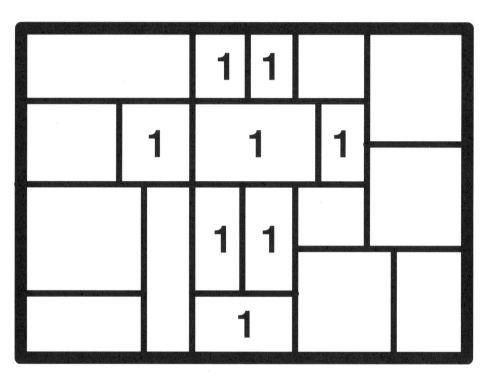

Answer is on page 236.

Patience

Patience leads to good things.
It is good to wait quietly.
~Lamentations 3:26

Patience Pays Off

The sweet, fresh-baked smell of chocolate chip cookies filled the air. Kira, and her little cousin, Steven, couldn't wait to eat them. They had taken turns making the cookie dough, adding ingredients to the bowl and stirring it until the dough was ready to bake. Now they had to wait the long fifteen minutes until the cookies were finished baking.

Steven hadn't wanted to wait. He wanted to enjoy the dough uncooked. Kira knew that if they were patient, they would soon have lots and lots of soft, sweet, gooey cookies to eat. So they stood together at the oven window.

As they watched the cookies bake, Kira held her arm around Steven as if to help him be patient. And their patience paid off! The timer chimed. The cookies were done! Kira and Steven ate, and ate, and ate. They were both so happy that they had been patient.

It can be hard to be patient when you want something, but Jesus teaches that having patience is a good thing. He says that if you wait patiently for Him, He will help you (Psalm 40:1).

Your Turn

1. How did being patient "pay off" for Kira and Steven?
2. Does Jesus teach that patience is a good or bad thing?
3. Why is it hard to be patient sometimes?

_____

_____

_____

_____

_____

_____

Prayer

Help me to be patient, Jesus, trusting in You to decide when things should happen. Amen.

Patient Growth

Read this to your child: "Waiting for cookies to bake requires a lot of patience, but waiting for a plant to grow takes even more. Test your patience. Plant a seed and wait for it to sprout and grow."

What You Need
- container
- decorations (optional)
- potting soil
- seeds (preferably corn)
- water

What to Do
Save an empty milk container, a soup can or some other container. Decorate the container if you like, fill with dirt, plant a seed (corn grows quite fast) and water. Set the can in the sun, and wait for yet another of God's quiet miracles to appear.

Curiosity

Curiosity is a gift from God, so you must use it wisely.
Knowledge will be pleasant to your soul.

~Proverbs 2:10

Curious Barbie

The truck was so big and loud! The kids watched through the living room windows as the orange truck drove its heavy load of concrete around the house. Daddy had been wanting to build a concrete porch on the back of the house, and today was the day.

The kids all pressed against the glass door, watching as the truck's driver carefully put the truck's shoot right in front of the glass where they were standing. Mom told Barbie that she shouldn't go so close to the glass because she might get scared, but Barbie wouldn't listen. Mom told Barbie "no", but Barbie was too curious to stay back.

Suddenly the truck's motor got very loud, and a whole bunch of gray, mushy concrete started running down the shoot and onto the ground where Daddy wanted the porch to be. The loudness of the truck, and the sight of all that gooey concrete pouring out, scared Barbie just as Mom had warned her it might. Pressing her face and hands against the glass, Barbie squeezed her eyes shut and screamed as loud as she could, tears and drool running down her face.

Curiosity is good. It makes you interested in things so that you learn more. But you need to remember that even if you're very curious about something, it's still not OK to do something naughty, like disobey your mom. You must obey what your parents, and Jesus, tell you to do. They know what is best for you.

Your Turn

1. How did Barbie's curiosity get her in trouble?
2. Why should Barbie have obeyed her mother?
3. Can you give an example of a time when you were curious about something?

_____

_____

_____

_____

Prayer

Thank You, Jesus, for the wonderful gift of curiosity that helps me learn more. Amen.

Bathing Barbie

Read this to your child: "Jesus wants you to use your curiosity to learn new things. Barbie used the curiosity God gave her in a bad way. She did a very naughty thing and had to take a bath. Color this picture of Barbie getting cleaned up."

Doubt

You should never doubt God.
God has said, "Never will I leave you."
~Hebrews 13:5

Who Made the Storm?

Christopher and Felicia sat in front of the TV, nervously watching the weather report. There was a scary storm moving through their area. Sudden flashes of lightning lit the darkness of the living room, loud booming thunder rattled the windows and the rain poured down in sheets. A tornado had been sighted not far away, and Christopher was very worried. As they sat listening to the storm warning, Felicia said to Christopher, "God makes a storm."

"Well, actually," replied Christopher, "storms are only black puffy clouds that got watered on when God planted a plant."

"God made everything, Christopher," Felicia corrected, and she went on to explain how tornadoes are made.

"Mom," called Christopher, "Felicia thinks tornadoes are fingers from God when He's digging, and they're really just wind that swirls around and around."

"Now, Christopher," Mom said, "you know that what Felicia thinks isn't exactly true, but the important thing to remember is that God made everything and we must never doubt that."

It can be easy to doubt sometimes that God made everything. Things you imagine and stories you hear my be fun to talk about, but the truth will always be that God made everything and everyone, and that never changes.

Your Turn

1. Do you like Christopher and Felicia's funny stories about how storms and tornadoes are made?
2. Did God make everything, or just some things?
3. Should we ever doubt God?

_____

_____

_____

_____

Prayer

Thank you Jesus for all the things that You made for us, even the scary ones like storms and tornadoes. Amen.

Creation

Read this to your child: "Color the pictures, and then circle the pictures that are of things God made. Is there anything that God didn't make?"

Teaching/Learning

We should try new things and keep learning.
Teach me knowledge.
~Psalm 119:66

Keep Learning!

"Where's the light?" Daddy asked Brea.

"Gah. Oooh," said Brea, pointing up to the ceiling above him.

"That's electricity making those lights work," said Daddy as he and Brea sat on the kitchen floor. Baby Brea gazed up at the ceiling light, a silent look of awe on her face as her daddy very seriously explained how electricity works. For a long time, Daddy talked about how the switch on the wall makes the light come on, why the light is so bright and why lights are such a good thing.

At such a young age, Daddy knew it was unlikely that Brea would understand much of what she was being taught. However, Daddy also knew that it's important to teach children all the time.

It's just as important to never tell yourself that you "can't" learn something new. You may sometimes give up or don't even try to learn something because you think you're not smart enough. Jesus wants you to use all that He has given you, and a way you can do that is to try new things—even when you think they might be beyond your abilities.

Your Turn

1. What were Daddy and Brea doing?
2. Why was Daddy teaching Brea about electricity?
3. When was the last time you tried to learn something that other people thought you weren't able to?

_____

_____

_____

_____

_____

Prayer

Jesus, help me to keep learning all the time, and as much as I can. I want to do my best to use all that You have given me. Amen.

Longer and Shorter

Read this to your child: "Jesus wants you to use all of the abilities He has given you to learn as much as you can, even when it is hard to do. This might seem hard at first, but if you try really hard, you'll figure it out!"

Which of these animals is the longest?

Which is the shortest?

You made it — congratulations! Now color the pictures.

Answer is on page 236.

Perseverance

Never give up.
Do not abandon the works of your hands.

~Psalm 138:8

Try Again

"I can't do it. Look, Mom, I'm just a little kid," said Tammy. Learning to tie her shoes had turned out to be harder than she thought.

"You know, Tammy" replied Mom, "your friend Kelsey knows how to tie her shoes already, and she's younger than you are. You need to try harder."

Tammy pulled at the laces on her black and white sneakers, and once again looped, crossed over and tugged on them, but it just wouldn't work. The laces were knotted, but not tied correctly.

"Try again" Mom urged. Tammy tried, and tried, and tried again. After trying many times and failing to do it, Tammy was ready to give up...but she didn't. She kept trying until finally, after a lot of practicing, she did it! She was so proud of herself. She grinned from ear to ear as she showed her Mom and sister her new accomplishment.

Tammy learned that even if something is hard to do, you can do it if you just keep trying. Lots of things take practice before you can do them. Getting dressed all by yourself, brushing your own teeth, combing your hair and tying your shoes are all important everyday things that you need to try over and over before you can really do them well. If you don't try, and keep trying, you'll never get better. Jesus wants you to always try your best.

Your Turn

1. What was Tammy trying to learn to do?
2. Would Tammy have learned to tie her shoes if she had given up after the first time she tried to do it?
3. Can you remember a time when you learned to do something only after practicing it over and over again?

_____

_____

_____

_____

_____

Prayer

Please help me, Jesus, to always try my best and never give up trying to learn new things. Amen.

Shapes

Read this to your child: "Whether it is tying your shoes, or even something easier, Jesus always wants you to try your best. If you keep practicing, and never give up, you can get better at doing even hard things. One thing that takes practice is drawing pretty shapes. A nice way to practice is by using cookie cutters. Just trace around a cookie cutter onto construction paper (or regular paper) and then color the shape in. Here are some fun cookie cutter shapes to practice."

Judgment

You shouldn't blindly trust others.
A prudent man gives thought to his steps.

~Proverbs 14:15

Open the Door!

Never open the door without permission—that was a house rule. Hannah knew the rule. She knew that it was for safety reasons that she was not to open the door without permission. Only Mom or Dad were able to tell if the person at the door was a friend and should be let into the house.

One day, as she was taking out the garbage, Mom accidentally locked herself out of the house. As Mom knocked on the door, Hannah left the blocks she was playing with and came to see who was there.

"Who is it?" Hannah asked.

"It's me," answered Mom. "Please open the door."

After a pause, Hannah said, "I'm not supposed to open the door without permission" and she ran off shouting, "Mom, Mom?"

Mom knocked on the door again, this time harder and louder. When Hannah finally came back to the door, she once again stated the house rule.

"But Hannah," answered Mom, "it's Mom! It's very good that you remember the rule, but this time it really is me, and you can let me in."

After a moment of silence, Mom heard the sound of a chair being slid to the door as Hannah climbed up to look through the peep-hole. Seeing that it really was Mom, Hannah finally let her in.

Hannah didn't allow herself to be distracted by the fact that the person at the door sounded like her mother. She carefully checked who was at the door before she opened it. Hannah did what she knew was right.

Just like the rules at Hannah's house, Jesus has set rules to follow. Many things will test your ability to follow these rules. You should never blindly trust what people tell you, because some people may try to trick you. Instead, just like Hannah, you must carefully check things out, trusting only in God's rules to guide you.

Your Turn

1. Why didn't Hannah open the door the first time Mom asked her to?
2. Why did Hannah finally decide to open the door for her mom?
3. Why is it important to follow the rules set for you?

Prayer

Thank You, Jesus, for all of the rules in my life that help me to be safe and happy. Please help me remember to think things through carefully and follow the rules You've set for my life. Amen.

Rules to Follow

Read this to your child: "Jesus has very clear rules for you in the Bible. It is important that you follow these rules, as well as the ones set by your parents, because Jesus wants you to live a safe and happy life. Here are some things you should think carefully about before doing. Color the pictures and then discuss with your parents why you should be careful in these situations."

Failure

Failure makes us work harder.
Do not be discouraged.

~Joshua 8:1

Keep Trying

"Why won't it open?" wondered Joyce. She tugged and pulled on the kitchen cabinet door, but it would only open a teeny-weeny amount. She couldn't get it open. Something was stopping it. Sliding her fingers along the top of the cabinet, Joyce found a small plastic latch. Aha! Mom had put that there to keep her from getting into the cupboard!

For the next month, Joyce carefully studied the cabinet latch whenever she thought Mom wasn't watching. Each time she tried to open it she would fail. She tried, and tried again, but still she failed to get the door open. Mom secretly watched as Joyce did her best to open the cabinet door, and thought that she would get discouraged and give up soon, but she never did. Each time she failed to open the door she seemed all the more determined to get into the cabinet. Failure just seemed to make her want to open the door even more.

Sometimes failure can be a good thing. Just like with Joyce, failure can make you work harder to succeed. Everything that happens to you happens for a reason. When you fail, Jesus may be actually helping you by making you work harder. The next time you can't do something, remember that it might be good that you failed the first time, and don't give up.

Your Turn

1. What did Joyce fail to do?
2. Why did Joyce keep trying?
3. Is failure always a bad thing? When is it good?

_____

_____

_____

_____

Prayer

Jesus, please help me to remember that failure isn't always a bad thing, and thank You for encouraging me to work harder. Amen.

Create a Shape

Read this to your child: "Even failure is a gift from Jesus. It makes you work harder for what you want. This might seem hard, but don't give up! Connect the numbers in order, from 1 to 4. What's the name of the shape you made? When you're done, you can color the pretty pictures."

Planning

There's enough time for both work and
play if you plan your time wisely.
Many are the plans in a man's heart.

~Proverbs 19:21

Wasted Time

"If we get our work done this morning, we can go shopping," said Mom. Frederick, Emily and Julie hurried to get dressed, make their beds and pick up their toys. While the children were hurrying, Mom finished the housework and got ready to leave.

Suddenly, Mom noticed that Frederick, Emily and Julie weren't doing their work anymore. They were playing.

"Hey, you guys," said Mom, "you'd better hurry up. We won't be able to go to the store if you don't get your jobs done before noon."

Throughout the morning Mom reminded the children of what they still needed to do, but they just kept playing. By the time noon arrived, the children were still playing and the work wasn't done. When they heard that they couldn't go to the store, the children were upset.

"But I want to go to the store," cried Emily.

"Can't we just go to the store anyway?" asked Frederick.

"We can do our work tomorrow," added Emily, as Julie threw down her shoes and screamed in protest.

Mom explained, "I told you what needed to be done if you wanted to go to the store, and you didn't do it. You made your choice."

If you plan your days carefully, you can do so much more. Frederick, Emily and Julie wasted a lot of time playing when they should have been doing their jobs. If they had gotten their work done, they would have had time to do something fun.

Jesus wants you to make good use of the time He gives you. If you carefully plan your days and your life, you will have plenty of time for both work and play, and use God's time wisely.

Your Turn

1. What did the children have to do if they wanted to go the store?
2. Why didn't the children get to go to the store?
3. Can you remember when you wasted too much time?

_____

_____

Prayer

Dear Jesus, please help me to never waste any of the precious time You give me. Amen.

Our Chores

Read this to your child: "Jesus doesn't want you to waste time. When you make good use of your time, like by helping others or doing your chores, it makes Jesus happy. Here are some jobs kids are supposed to do sometimes. Circle the ones that you've helped your mommy and daddy with, then color the pictures."

Questioning

We should question everything except God's love.
Give...a discerning heart...to
distinguish between right and wrong.

~1 Kings 3:9

Slaying Dragons

"Where are you goin' dad?" asked Julie as she watched her daddy put on a pair of shoes and coat.

"I'm going to slay a dragon," Daddy responded.

Julie thought for a moment about what Daddy had said and then answered, "Dragons can't live in the cold, Daddy."

"Well maybe there's a warm spot in the woods where a dragon lives, and maybe that's where I'm going," said Daddy.

Again, Julie thought a moment about what her daddy had told her. She thought Daddy might be teasing her, but the idea that a dragon might be living in the woods was very exciting. Could it possibly be true? Finally, Julie made up her mind. "Now look, Dad, no you're not," Julie said. "Where are you going?"

"To slay a dragon," Daddy simply said.

"Dad! You're just teasing me," Julie insisted.

Daddy started laughing. He was very happy that Julie was smart enough to know that she was just being teased.

The Bible says that you should question everything, except the love of God. Jesus wants you to think about things and not just blindly believe what people tell you. In this story, Julie's daddy was just teasing her, but Julie still carefully thought through and questioned what Daddy was saying to her. Just like Julie, you need to think about everything, using the intelligence that Jesus has given you to decide what's true and what isn't.

Your Turn

1. What did Julie's daddy say he was going outside to do?
2. Why did Julie question what her daddy told her?
3. How did Julie know that her daddy was just teasing her?

_____

_____

_____

Prayer

Please help me, Jesus, to think carefully about everything I'm told, and only completely trust Your Word. Amen.

Real or Fake?

Read this to your child: "One thing you should never question is God's love. Questioning is a good way to learn. Ask your mom or dad if you are not sure which of the following are real. Draw a line under the things that are 'real,' then color them."

Answer is on page 236.

 # Confusion

You shouldn't let your frustrations keep you
from trying to learn new things.
Make the most of every opportunity.

~Colossians 4:5

Finding the Answer

"What's the answer, Charlotte?" Mom asked as they sat on the couch studying a preschool workbook. Charlotte was trying her best to figure out what should come next in a series of things. She looked at the page in front of her and studied it as hard as she could, but no matter how hard she tried, she just couldn't get the right answer.

"I don't know," said Charlotte. "I don't know what the answer is."

Charlotte tried again, looking at each picture carefully, but she just couldn't figure it out. Finally, Charlotte hit the page with her pencil. "I don't know!" she cried again.

Charlotte was confused and frustrated by the question in the workbook. She hadn't learned how to figure out that kind of problem, so she didn't know the answer.

Lots of things in life are like that. No matter how old you are, or how many things you learn, there are still always some things that you don't know yet. Just like Charlotte, you can be confused and frustrated when you don't know the answer to something. What's important is that you don't give up. If you keep trying, someday you'll find the answer you're looking for.

Of course, Jesus is always the best answer. Turn to Him when you are confused and He will help you.

Your Turn

1. Why was Charlotte confused and frustrated?
2. Why is it important to never give up trying to learn new things?
3. Can you think of something that you know now, but that was really hard for you to learn?

_____

_____

_____

_____

Prayer

Please help me, Jesus, to never give up no matter how hard something is. Amen.

Which Is Next?

Read this to your child: "You can always turn to Jesus when you are confused. Even if something is hard to do, just keep working at it and Jesus will help you figure it out. Here's a problem like the one in Charlotte's workbook that she had trouble answering. Can you figure out the answer? Which should be next in this series, the triangle or the circle? Can you do this next one too? Is the flower next, or the lady bug?"

Answer is on page 236.

God Is in Control

Fear

Don't let fear stop you from doing the right thing.
So do not fear...I will strengthen you and help you.

~Isaiah 41:10

The Power of Fear

Alan and Brittany were making cookie cut-outs. They were especially excited because Mom was letting them use the big, marble rolling pin to roll out the dough. They pushed the rolling pin forward and pulled it back, over and over again, watching the dough become smooth and flat.

They were almost ready to put down the rolling pin and start using the cookie-cutters when the rolling pin fell off the table. It hit the floor with a loud thud, and left a small dent in the vinyl floor.

Neither Brittany nor Alan wanted to tell Mom what happened because they were afraid of being punished. When Mom asked them what happened they said, "Nothing." They allowed their fear to keep them from doing the right thing.

When Mom finally discovered what had happened, Brittany and Alan were punished — not because they dropped the rolling pin, but because they didn't tell the truth.

Have you ever been so afraid that you didn't tell the truth? Jesus teaches that you should always try your best to do what is right, even when you're afraid. You should never allow fear, or anything else, to keep you from doing what you know is right. Jesus should be your only guide in deciding what you should do.

Your Turn

1. What did Alan and Brittany lie to their mom about?
2. Do you think Alan and Brittany wished they had told their mom what happened? Why or why not?
3. Can you think of a time when you were so afraid that you didn't do the right thing?

_____

_____

_____

Prayer

Jesus, please help me to always remember that You are with me, even when I'm afraid. Give me the strength to still do what is right, even when I'm scared. Amen.

Cookie Cut-Outs

Children love to bake cookies, and your kids will love it even more when they make their own cookie cutters. Have your children draw whatever shape they like on a piece of cardboard and cut it out with safety scissors. Laying the picture on the dough, your child can trace around it with a butter knife (which also promotes coordination skills). Just as Jesus guides your child's life, the cookie cutter will guide your child's knife. As your child cuts out the shape, talk about how Jesus' guidance in her life can help her to do the right thing, even when she is afraid or unsure of what to do next. Here are some suggested "cookie cutter" shapes for your child to color.

Guilt

Guilt tells you when you've done something wrong.
*Anyone...who knows the good he ought
to do and doesn't do it, sins.*

~James 4:17

Eaten Up with Guilt

Umm, the cookies tasted so good! Two-year-old Annie couldn't believe how wonderful the soft, chewy cookies felt in her mouth, or how sweet and gooey the chocolate chips were as she licked them with her tongue.

Mom had just baked a whole batch of her special, crunchy chocolate chip oatmeal cookies and left them on the kitchen counter to cool. Mom told Annie that the cookies were for a special occasion and that she must not eat any, but Annie sneaked into the kitchen anyway. She only meant to eat just one, but then they tasted so good! How could she stop herself?

First one cookie was gone, then another, then another, and soon all two dozen cookies were either all or partly eaten. Now Annie felt very, very full. A few minutes later, Mom walked into the kitchen. It only took one look at Annie to know exactly what had happened.

There Annie stood, brown chocolate goo coating every finger, and a guilty face spotted with small cookie crumbs and smeared chocolate. Even the end of Annie's nose had oatmeal on it from her feast.

Mom said, "Oh, no." In that moment Annie learned the meaning of guilt. She would never be able to undo the damage that she had done, and she felt awful. Jesus gives you the feeling of guilt when you need to ask for forgiveness. He forgives you when you are truly sorry for what you have done. Annie felt bad. That's how she knew that what she had done was wrong. Now that Annie felt guilty, she was also able to feel sorry for what she had done and ask for forgiveness.

Your Turn

1. What did Annie do that was wrong?
2. Why did Annie feel guilty?
3. Can you think of a time when you felt guilty about doing something you shouldn't have?

_____

_____

_____

Prayer

Jesus, thank You for the feeling of guilt that helps me to know when I've done something wrong. Amen.

Color and Count

Read this to your child: "Here are some of the chocolate chip oatmeal cookies that Annie loves so much. Can you count how many there are? After you're done counting, you can color them." As your child colors, remind her that even something as little as taking a cookie when she is not supposed to is wrong in Jesus' eyes.

 # Worry

You can control your fears.
The mind controlled by the Spirit is life and peace.
~Romans 8:6

Bad Dreams

"Now what?" Daddy said as he heard feet running down the hallway. The children had been asleep for hours, and Mom and Dad had just gone to bed themselves.

"Daddy, I had a bad dream," called Megan as she peeked around the bedroom door. "I'm scared."

"Ooh, poor Megan," said Daddy. "Come get in bed between us."

Megan smiled and quickly climbed up the side of the bed, over Mom, and plopped down into the space between her parents. "I was dreaming about bats. They were coming to bite me."

"Don't worry, Megan," comforted Mom. "Bad dreams are scary, but they can't really hurt you."

"But I'm afraid the bad dream will come back," cried Megan.

"Well, worrying about it won't help," said Mom. "Just think happy thoughts now, and maybe you'll have happy dreams."

Worrying about something won't make it go away. The best way to deal with your fear is to do something to stop what you're afraid of. If you place yourself in Jesus' hands, and set your thoughts on love and goodness, Jesus will guide and protect you.

Megan learned that worrying about her bad dream wasn't going to stop it from happening. By thinking happy thoughts instead, she was able to sleep through the night without the bat dream coming back to scare her.

Your Turn

1. Why was Megan afraid?
2. What did Megan do to stop being afraid?
3. How do you keep from being afraid?

_____

_____

_____

Prayer

Thank You, Jesus, for giving me the power to control my fears. Please keep me in Your care. Amen.

Bat Dreams

Read this to your child: "Jesus helps us overcome our fears. Just as Jesus guided Megan to have happy thoughts, let these dots guide you to see what Megan was scared of in her dream. When you're done, you can color it."

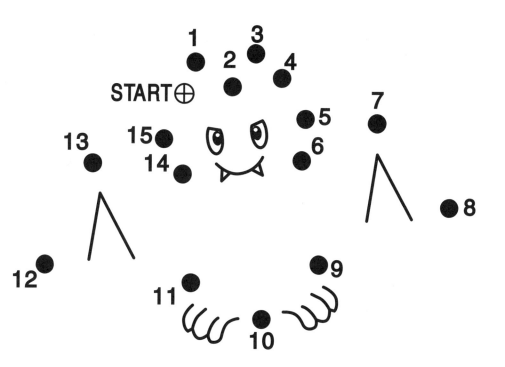

Answer is on page 236.

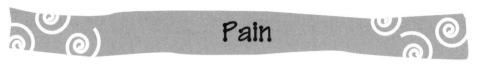

Pain

Sometimes pain is necessary.
They spit on him, and...struck Him on the head.
~Matthew 27:30

Jesus Understands Your Pain

Three-year-old Bethany had a small bump on her earlobe. It didn't hurt, but the doctor still said that it had to be taken off. The doctor called it a cyst and said that it was nothing to worry about, but Bethany was still worried. Being in the doctor's office wasn't any fun, and she was afraid that taking the cyst off her earlobe was going to hurt.

The doctor's office was cold, and the table that Bethany had to lie on was hard. A big, bright light was above her. Bethany would have been more scared if she hadn't seen Mom, Dad and her brother Scott beside her. When the doctor used his small, sharp knife to cut the cyst out of her earlobe, it hurt a lot, and Bethany screamed. Even though the doctor was all done in just a couple of seconds, Bethany still felt a lot of pain. It felt like someone was pinching her earlobe really hard. She cried a lot.

Have you ever felt something hurt a whole lot? Jesus knows what it's like to feel pain. When He died for you on the cross He felt a lot of pain, but He did it because He loves you so much. Sometimes you need to feel some pain, but you can always feel a little better when you're hurting if you remember that Jesus is always with you, helping you through your pain. He understands what it's like.

Your Turn

1. What do you think Bethany was thinking while she was in the doctor's office?
2. When is the last time you felt a lot of pain?
3. What can make you feel better when you're hurt?

_____

_____

_____

_____

Prayer

Dear Jesus, please help me to always remember that You are with me to help me through anything. Amen.

Facing Pain

Read this to your child: "When Jesus died on the cross for our sins He suffered a lot of pain, but He did it because He wanted to save us all from a lot of pain in the future. Bethany also had so suffer some pain in order to avoid a lot of pain in the future. Knowing that Jesus understands what it is like to feel pain helped her to get through it."

Draw Bethany's face before she went to the doctor.

Draw Bethany's face after she want to the doctor.

How do you think she's feeling now?

Anger

Don't let anger cause you to do something bad.
In your anger do not sin.
~Ephesians 4:26

Angry Choices

Becky was so angry! How could Mom put her in the house when all of the other kids were still outside playing, she thought. It wasn't fair! She decided right then and there that she would get even.

Becky went straight to the china cabinet and opened the doors. She knew she was never ever allowed to go near Mom's china cabinet, but she was so angry that she did it anyway. Reaching inside she began to pull out first one, then another and another of Mom's fancy china plates and serving platters. One by one she smashed them on the floor with all her might, breaking them into a million pieces, and denting the wooden floor.

When Mom came in the house a moment later she was shocked by what she saw. Becky was surrounded by broken china. Becky couldn't understand why Mom looked so frightened and worried as she swooped Becky up in her arms and began to check her all over for cuts. Mom was so happy to find Becky wasn't hurt that she forgot to be angry.

Becky was confused. She thought she would feel better if she showed Mom how angry she was, but instead she had scared and upset her mom. Becky didn't feel better at all. In fact, she felt worse.

Have you ever done something because you were angry, and then later wished you hadn't done it? It's OK to feel angry sometimes, but it's not OK to do bad things just because you're feeling angry. Jesus taught that love and understanding are better than anger.

Your Turn

1. Why did Becky get so angry?
2. Why did Becky break her mom's dishes?
3. Can you remember a time when you were so angry that you did something you shouldn't have?

_____

_____

_____

_____

Prayer

Please help me, Jesus, to never make choices out of anger, but rather out of love and understanding. Amen.

Erupting Anger

Read this to your child: "Jesus gave us anger just like He gave us all of our other feelings. Anger isn't a bad thing; it's what we do with our anger that Jesus may not like. Just like an erupting volcano, if you express your anger appropriately, your anger will bubble up and out and flow away."

What You Need
- 2 tablespoons baking soda
- 1/2 cup vinegar
- 2 cups flour or dirt

What to Do
Make a tall hill of the flour or dirt. Form a deep well in the center of the hill and put the baking soda in it. Pour in the vinegar and watch the "volcano" erupt. Tell your child to imagine her own angry or hurt feelings as you watch your volcano erupt, then your child may color the picture below.

Remorse

Feeling bad tells you you've done something wrong.
*Anyone...who knows the good he ought
to do and doesn't do it, sins.*

~James 4:17

Painting Day

Painting day! Darlene loved painting day. She loved the bright paints and the way the water in her cup would change colors when she dipped her brush in. While Mom worked at her desk, Darlene sat at the kitchen table happily painting a picture of her house.

Then suddenly Darlene thought, "Wait a minute. It's boring just painting on paper. I'm going to paint a picture on the table instead."

Darlene began to paint a lovely picture on top of the kitchen table, but then she thought, "Wait a minute. It would be even more fun to paint a picture on the kitchen wall." So Darlene painted a picture on the wall, and then on the floor, and then on herself.

When Mom saw what Darlene had done she was very angry, and disappointed in Darlene. Mom took away Darlene's paint set and sent her to the time-out corner.

As she sat in the corner, Darlene thought about what she had done and wished she had never painted on places she wasn't supposed to.

Have you ever done something and then later wished you hadn't done it? Darlene didn't just feel bad for what she had done. She felt "remorse"— she wished she had never done it at all.

Feeling bad about something is one of the best ways you can know that you've done something wrong. Feelings like guilt and remorse are ways that Jesus helps you to be the best that you can be.

Your Turn

1. Why did Darlene paint places that she shouldn't have?
2. Do you think that Darlene would do the same bad thing again?
3. Can you remember a time when you did something bad, and then wished you had never done it at all?

_____

_____

Prayer

Thank You, Jesus, for Your gift of remorse. Wishing that I had never done a bad thing helps me to never make the same mistake twice. Amen.

Paint a Paper Plate

Read this to your child: "Jesus made Darlene feel remorse to show her that she had done something bad. Darlene would not have felt remorse if she had used the painting talents Jesus gave her in a good way. Here is a way to do some painting in a good way."

What You Need

- non-toxic paints or crayons
- paper plates
- construction paper, cut into strips
- safety scissors
- non-toxic glue or tape
- string or yarn

What to Do

Instruct your child to decorate the paper plate and strips of paper. Affix the paper strips to the plate and attach the string through a hole at the top. Now you're ready to hang your plate indoors, or outside when it can blow in the wind (just don't leave it out in the rain or overnight).

Change

The only thing that doesn't change is Jesus.
Jesus Christ is the same yesterday and today and forever.
~Hebrews 13:8

Change Is Normal

"But we never do it that way," pleaded Brenna. "You always send me to the corner when I'm bad."

Brenna was upset because Mom was changing her punishment for doing something wrong. Now instead of being sent to the corner, she was having one of her privileges taken away—like no TV for the rest of the day, or going to bed early.

"But can't you just send me to the corner instead?" asked Brenna.

Mom explained, "Now that you're older, Brenna, you need to have punishments that older kids would have. After all, you're not a baby anymore."

Brenna didn't like that her punishment was changing. Some changes, however, did make her happy—like when she got a special surprise for her birthday. Whether change is good or bad, happy or sad, it is a normal part of life. The only thing that will never change, Jesus tells us, is His love. Jesus is always the same. No matter how many things in your life change, Jesus is always with you.

Your Turn

1. Why was Brenna upset?
2. Why do you think Brenna wanted to go to the corner instead of having a privilege taken away?
3. Has there been a change in your life lately that you didn't like?

_____

_____

_____

_____

_____

Prayer

Jesus, sometimes things change and I do not like it. I know I can always count on You to be here when I need You. Thank You, Jesus, for not changing. Amen.

Sprouting Change

Read this to your child: "Jesus' love never changes, but He does change the things around you all of the time. A good way to see how quickly Jesus changes things in nature is by watching seeds sprout."

What You Need

- birdseed or sunflower seeds
- wet paper towels folded on a plate
- plastic wrap

What to Do

Sprinkle some birdseed (sunflower seeds work especially well) on a wet paper towel that has been folded in fourths and placed it on a plate (check once a day to make sure the paper towel is still wet). Cover the plate with plastic wrap. In about 48 hours the seeds will start to sprout. Your child will think it is a lot of fun to see what normally happens underground!

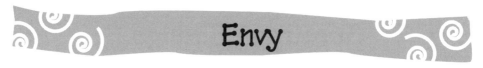

Envy

Jealousy won't get you what you need.
A heart at peace gives life to the body, but envy rots the bones.
~Proverbs 14:30

Pulling Teeth

Bruce's second tooth just came out. The tooth fairy left one dollar under his pillow.

Bruce's little sister, Polly, was very jealous of Bruce. She wanted the tooth fairy to visit her, too. She wanted to have her tooth come out.

Mom explained to Polly that she was too little yet to be losing her teeth, and she must never pull on them. They would come out by themselves when they were ready.

The next day, while Bruce was at kindergarten, Polly began to pull on one of her teeth. She pulled and pulled, but it didn't budge. She tried to wiggle it back and forth, but it wouldn't move. Then she tried to bang on her tooth with Bruce's toy pliers, but it still was as tight as ever. None of her teeth would loosen up. She was very sad. Now not only didn't she have a tooth to give to the tooth fairy, but all that pulling on her teeth had made her mouth sore.

Polly learned that doing something out of jealousy usually doesn't get you what you want, and can actually make things worse. She should have waited until she was older, like Mom told her to, instead of trying to force her teeth to loosen up before they were ready.

Polly should have been happy with how God made her, instead of wanting to be like someone else. Jesus made everyone special and unlike anyone else. You should be thanking Jesus for who you are and not be jealous of others.

Your Turn

1. Why was Polly jealous of Bruce?
2. Why was Polly wrong to be jealous of Bruce?
3. Can you remember a time when you were jealous of someone else?

_____

_____

_____

Prayer

Thank You, Jesus, for making me special. Help me to never be jealous of others. Amen.

The Right Face

Read this to your child: "Jesus made us all different. You should thank Jesus for making everyone special." Ask your child to circle the picture that is different from the others. Then have your child fill in the rest of the picture.

Answer is on page 236.

Adaptability

Jesus makes all change for the good.
God works for the good of those who love him.

~Romans 8:28

An Ever-Changing World

Two-year-old Nikki stood up on her tip-toes as far as she could and stretched her neck to see what was on top of the kitchen counter. She could barely see the cookie jar, the coffee maker and the phone. She was certain there must be many more wonderful things up there. Oh, if she could only reach the counter-top!

Nikki had always been too little to reach the kitchen counter, but now she wondered if maybe she could climb there. She slowly, quietly slid one of the kitchen stools over to the counter, and carefully climbed to the top. She was a little scared to be up so high, but she really, really wanted to get to all that fun stuff on the counter. Nikki carefully stood up on the stool and found a whole new world. She played with the coffee-maker, pushed all the buttons on the phone, took just one bite out of each cookie in the cookie jar, and wiped her nose with the kitchen towel.

Oh how happy she was...until Mom found out. From that day forward, all of the stools were kept upside-down, at least until Nikki learned to set them back up. No one in the family liked it that way. It was hard for the other kids to always turn their chairs over when they were done using them, but it had to be done.

Sometimes you have to change how you live so that everyone can be happier. Like Nikki, people or things in your life will change. If you can adapt, or change along with them, your life will be easier and happier. Jesus makes all change for the good, and even though it may not seem that way sometimes, you must trust Him.

Your Turn

1. Why did everyone have to start keeping the kitchen chairs upside-down?
2. When was the last time you had to change what you usually do?
3. Why shouldn't you worry about changes in our lives?

_____

_____

_____

Prayer

Jesus, I want to always remember that You only change things for the good. Help me to trust You. Amen.

Changing Colors

Read this to your child: "Jesus changes things in your life to make the world a better place for you. Here are some things that change. Color them and think about how these things have changed for you."

Sadness

It's OK to feel sad sometimes.
You lifted me out of the depths.

~Psalm 30:1

Rainy Daze

Amanda had just heard that she couldn't play outside for the rest of the day. The weather had turned cold, and it was starting to rain. "But I like rain," complained Amanda. "I don't care if I get wet."

"I said no, Amanda," Mom said firmly. "It's not good for you to go out in this kind of weather."

Amanda pressed her forehead against the glass window as she looked out. She could see the rain pouring down, forming little puddles on the gravel driveway. How she would love to splash in those puddles!

"Oh well," Amanda said with a sigh, "maybe I'll go out tomorrow." Amanda didn't like how she was feeling. Nothing else sounded like fun. She only wanted to play outside, but she couldn't. She was sad.

Sometimes, especially when things don't happen the way you'd like them to, you feel sad. It's OK to feel sad. It doesn't feel good to be sad, but it won't last forever. In time, your sadness will go away and you'll have fun again.

Maybe you can help your sadness go away faster if you tell Jesus how you're feeling. Jesus is always with you to help you…even on rainy days.

Your Turn

1. Why did Amanda feel sad?
2. What are some things Amanda could have done to make her sadness go away?
3. When was the last time you were sad?

_____

_____

_____

_____

_____

Prayer

Sometimes I feel sad, Jesus. Thank You for always being with me so I can tell You how I'm feeling. Amen.

Make Your Own Rain Gauge

Read this to your child: "Jesus does all things for your good. If something makes you sad, try to think of why Jesus made it happen. Amanda couldn't go outside when it rained, but the rain helped the flowers, trees and grass grow — making her world a healthier and more beautiful place. Rainy days can be more fun if you have a rain gauge to measure the amount of water that falls from the sky."

What You Need
- any transparent container (a glass jar works well)
- paper (regular or construction)
- safety scissors
- pen or pencil
- ruler
- tape

What to Do
Cut a thin strip of paper. Using a ruler as a guide, mark off 1 inch, 2 inches, etc. Tape the paper to the jar (make sure the tape completely covers the paper or the rain will destroy your mini-ruler). Place your jar outside in an open space. Either brace it with something so that the wind won't blow it over, or fit it into a shallow indentation in the dirt to hold it steady. Now you can anxiously await the next rainfall.

Needs

Jesus gives us all we need.
Those who 'trust God' lack nothing.
~Psalm 34:9

Judy's Flour Garden

Judy looked out the living room window. She could see the gray tower of a grain elevator off in the distance. Daddy explained to Judy that the tall tower is where farmers take their corn, wheat and other crops to be stored. "What do they do with that?" asked Judy.

"Well," Daddy began, "they make flour from wheat, which we use to make food. Food is something everyone needs."

"They make flour there?" Judy asked.

"The wheat they store there is made into flour," Daddy answered.

From that day on, whenever Judy saw the grain elevator, she always said, "That's my flower garden where they make flowers and cookies and cakes. It makes things we need."

Judy learned from her daddy that the grain elevator helped to make things people need. Jesus also makes things that people need. In fact, Jesus makes everything you need. He gave you life, and gives you everything you need to live your life in the best possible way.

Your Turn

1. Why did Judy call the grain elevator her "flower garden"?
2. What are grain elevators used for?
3. Who gives you everything we need?

_____

_____

_____

_____

_____

_____

_____

Prayer

Jesus, thank You for giving me life and everything I need. Amen.

Flour Power

Read this to your child: "Jesus gives us everything we need, including flour, which is used in many of the foods we eat."

Tell your child to circle the things below that are made with flour:

Tell your child to draw her favorite thing that she likes to make with flour:

Answer is on page 236.

Death

After we die, we will all be together again in Heaven.
Whoever...believes in me will never die.
~John 11:26

Will I Ever See Bluebird Again?

The room was very quiet. Usually when Jama woke up, she heard the shrill chirps of her pet parakeet, Bluebird. But this morning was different. There was no sound from the silver cage that hung in the corner.

Jama dashed across the living room to where Bluebird's cage hung, got up on her tip-toes, and stretched her neck to look into her pet's cage. Where was Bluebird? The cage was empty!

"Mom, Mom," Jama cried as she ran to the kitchen where her mother was preparing breakfast. "Mom, where is Bluebird? I can't find him."

Jama's mother kneeled down in front of her as she explained, "I'm sorry, honey," she said. "Bluebird died last night. He's gone to heaven now."

Jama's lower lip quivered as she exclaimed, "I want to see him. I want Bluebird right now!"

Jama's mother showed her the shoe box she had lovingly made into a casket to hold Bluebird's body, and there was Bluebird, lying perfectly still.   Together, Jama and her mother carried Bluebird to the back yard, where they prayed for her and buried her in the ground. Jama made a wooden cross out of toothpicks to mark her pet's grave. As she placed it in the ground over Bluebird's grave, she looked up at her mom with tears in her eyes and asked, "Will I ever see Bluebird again?" Mom hugged Jama and explained, "I don't know about Bluebird, honey, but Jesus teaches that when someone who loves Jesus dies, he goes to heaven to be with Jesus, and that someday we will all be together again in heaven with Jesus, too."

Your Turn

1. Why was Jama sad?
2. When someone dies, will we ever see them again?
3. Do you remember a time when someone you loved died? How did that make you feel?

_____

_____

_____

Prayer

Thank You, Jesus, for Your promise that we will all be with You in heaven after we die. Amen.

Toothpick Cross

Read this to your child: "The cross reminds us of Jesus' promise that we will all be together again someday in heaven. You can make your own cross now."

What You Need
- toothpicks (flat are best)
- non-toxic glue
- cardboard

What to Do
After smearing a thin coating of glue on the cardboard, your child can stick the toothpicks to it to make a variety of shapes, including a "toothpick cross."

Revenge

We should love and forgive others, and never act vengeful.
Do not seek revenge...but love your neighbor.

~Leviticus 19:18

Holly's Revenge

"No, no, no!" screamed Holly. She and Oliver were both sitting at the kitchen table eating breakfast. Holly forgot that she had already eaten her bacon, and thought Oliver had taken hers.

"No, no," yelled Holly again, pointing at Oliver's plate on the opposite side of the table.

"Holly," Mom reminded her, "you already ate your bacon. Stop bothering Oliver."

Mom pointed to Holly's plate, showing her that the bacon had been eaten, but Holly didn't believe her.

"No, no!" Holly continued, now standing on her chair as she stared at Oliver's breakfast plate. Holly was convinced that Oliver had stolen her bacon, and now she wanted revenge. Oliver did his best to ignore her, but suddenly Holly leapt onto the table, lunged forward and grabbed Oliver's bacon.

"Hey," Oliver hollered, "give that back!" But it was too late. As quickly as she had snatched it, Holly sat down and stuffed her mouth full. Holly had taken her revenge.

Holly had behaved very badly. Not only was she wrong about Oliver stealing her bacon, but she was also wrong to be vengeful. Jesus wants you to love and forgive others, not "get back" at people for what you think they've done to hurt you.

Your Turn

1. What did Holly do to Oliver?
2. Why did Holly take Oliver's bacon?
3. Even if Oliver had stolen Holly's bacon, would she have been right to take revenge on him?

Prayer

Dear Jesus, I want to be loving and forgiving of others, just as You've been to me. Please help me to remember that being vengeful is wrong. Amen.

Hungry Holly

Read this to your child: "Jesus teaches that you should leave revenge up to Him and be forgiving of others. What Holly did was wrong. Even though she took her brother's bacon, she was still hungry. Draw some food on her plate for her and then color the picture."

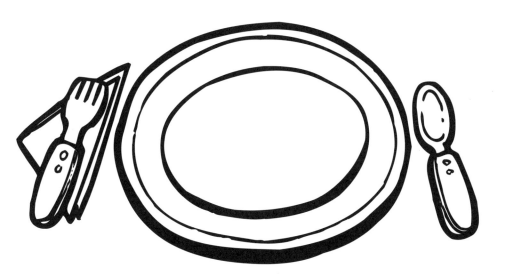

Hatred

It's OK to hate the bad things people do, but don't hate people.
Let those who love the Lord hate evil.

~Psalm 97:10

Kari's Bad Behavior

It was a fun day! All of the kids were outside painting a special banner for Daddy. Zachary and Belinda painted in the letters on the banner while Kari colored the big red heart in the center. Before long, the words "We love Daddy" were visible...but Zachary wasn't as happy as Mom thought he would be.

"What's the matter Zachary?" Mom asked.

"Kari keeps coloring where she's not supposed to," he answered. "I hate it when she does that." Zachary sat back and sighed as he watched two-year-old Kari color little spots here, there and everywhere...including on herself.

"Stop it, Kari!" Zachary yelled. "Why would you do such a thing?"

Kari looked up at Zachary briefly, made a shrill screeching sound at him, and then went back to drawing spots on her tummy with the red marking pen.

The Bible says to "hate evil" but love each other. You can learn from Jesus to love people, but still hate the bad things that people sometimes do. Zachary understands that Kari isn't bad even though she does bad things sometimes. He "hates" the bad things Kari does, but he never ever hates her.

Your Turn

1. Why was Zachary angry with Kari?
2. Did Zachary "hate" Kari, or just what she was doing?
3. Is it OK to hate people?

_____

_____

_____

_____

_____

Prayer

Jesus, please help me to remember that even though people sometimes do bad things, I should never hate them. It's only OK to hate the bad things they do. Amen.

Body Painting

Read this to your child: "Jesus taught that you should love people, even when you hate the things they do. Your mom may 'hate' it when you make a mess, but she still loves you. Here is a 'mess' you can make that your parents will love!"

What You Need
• non-toxic paints (or markers)
• poster board (or big sheets of paper, cardboard, paper bags, etc.)

What to Do
This is a particularly fun activity for a hot summer day. Put on your old bathing suits (those you don't mind staining), and use your hands, feet, legs, etc., to paint on your poster boards. After you're done, just use the garden hose to wash the paint off before you go inside. You could also do this in the basement or garage and then go straight to the tub to wash up when done.

Jealousy

Jealousy hurts friendships.
Who can stand before jealousy?
~Proverbs 27:4

Nothing Good Comes from Jealousy

Betsy loved her big sister, Patricia. Even though Patricia was two years older than her, Betsy enjoyed doing many of the same things. They often made tall towers with wooden blocks or played dress-up with Mom's clothes. Sometimes Patricia would even snuggle with Betsy on the couch and read her a story.

One day Patricia received a beautiful necklace from Grandma Helen as a birthday gift. It had pretty wooden beads and sparkled with all the colors of the rainbow. Patricia loved her necklace and wore it every day. Betsy also loved the necklace and would sometimes scream until Patricia would let her wear it for a while. Patricia was happy to share with Betsy, but for Betsy that wasn't enough. Betsy was jealous of Patricia. Betsy wanted the necklace for her very own.

One day Betsy screamed at Patricia to let her wear the necklace, but this time Patricia said no. Betsy, in a fit of jealous anger, grabbed the pretty necklace around Patricia's neck and yanked as hard as she could. The necklace broke and the beads fell to the floor, bouncing and rolling in every direction.

Betsy's jealousy had led her to be mean to Patricia. After breaking the necklace, it was a very long time until Patricia would play with Betsy again, which made Betsy very sad.

Nothing good ever comes out of jealousy. Jesus gives us all many special gifts, and we should be happy for what we have instead of jealous of what others have. Betsy learned that her jealousy over Patricia's necklace only caused trouble for both of them. The necklace was broken so no one could enjoy it now, and Betsy no longer had a friend to play with.

Your Turn

1. Why was Betsy jealous of Patricia?
2. What bad thing did Betsy do because of her jealousy?
3. Have you ever been jealous of someone?

Prayer

Please help me, Jesus, to not be jealous of others. Thank You for all the wonderful, special gifts that You have given me. Amen.

Make Your Own Paper Jewelry

Read this to your child: "It makes Jesus sad when you are jealous of others. He wants you to be thankful for all He has given you. Betsy should not have been jealous of Patricia's necklace. She could have made her own instead, and so can you! Just follow these instructions."

What You Need
- paper (colored or construction paper)
- safety scissors
- non-toxic crayons
- non-toxic glue
- string or yarn

What to Do
Instruct your child to decorate the paper and then cut it into strips of varying lengths and widths. Using a finger, smear a thin coating of glue on the paper and then fold over one end and roll the strip into the shape of a bead. When your "beads" are all done, string them onto a piece of yarn or string. You can also hook the rings together before you tape them to make a long chain if you like.

My Place in God's World

Rules

Rules are made to protect you.

The grace of God...teaches us to live
self-controlled, upright and godly lives.

~Titus 2:11-12

Rules Are Not Made to Be Broken

Up and down they rode. The escalator at the department store was one of Rae and Courtney's favorite things. They loved to ride on the moving staircase as it carried them to the second floor, and then ride the down escalator back again.

Courtney stood still as she rode the escalator and held onto the handrail. Rae however, didn't want to obey the safety rules. She asked Mom why she couldn't walk up and down the steps as they moved. Mom told her it was dangerous.

After they were finished shopping, Rae and Courtney talked Mom into letting them ride one last time. As the staircase carried them down to the first floor, Courtney carefully stepped off just as she was supposed to.

Rae, however, did not. When her step reached the bottom, Rae turned and hopped back up to the next one. She thought herself to be quite clever until her shoe caught on the edge of one of the rising steps and she started to fall. Mom reached out to catch her but it was too late. Rae fell flat on her back onto the escalator stairway. Rae's back and leg hurt, and she started to cry. She was also ashamed of her behavior as several people turned to look at her.

Rae got hurt on the escalator, but she learned a valuable lesson. Rules are made to protect you. When you ignore them you can get hurt.

In the same way, Jesus has set rules for you to live by. You can find those rules in the Bible. Even though the rules you learn in church and from your parents may not seem like much fun, they are there to protect you. You will live a happier, healthier life if you follow the rules Jesus has set.

Your Turn

1. Why didn't Rae follow the rules?
2. What happened to Rae when she didn't follow the rules?
3. Can you remember a time when you didn't follow the rules? What happened?

_____

_____

_____

_____

Prayer

Thank You, Jesus, for setting rules for me to follow. Please help me to remember that following Your rules is very important. Amen.

Up and Down

Read this to your child: "The most important rules you have are those that Jesus has given you. They teach you how to live your life. Instructions, rules and directions are all meant to make life easier. Rae and Courtney love to ride up and down on the escalator. Can you follow the instructions to show which balloon is up in these pictures and which is down? Color the balloons that are up. Draw an X over the ones that are down."

Answer is on page 236.

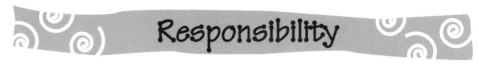

Responsibility

You should take good care of all you have been given.
And let them rule over...all the earth.

~Genesis 1:26

Clean Up Your Toys!

Krystal didn't want to pick up her toys. She didn't want to go to bed, either. In fact, Krystal didn't want to do anything that Mom was telling her to do.

When Mom said, "It's time for you to clean up your toys," Krystal asked, "Why?"

Mom explained, "Krystal, you know the house rules. When it's time for bed, it's time to clean up your toys. So clean up your toys now."

Krystal still didn't want to clean up, so she put on her best angry face and said, in her loudest voice, "No!"

Mom took Krystal by the arm and led her quickly to the time-out corner. But even though she had been punished, Krystal still would not do her job. Mom told her, "Krystal, if you won't put your toys away, maybe you're not responsible enough yet to have toys." Then Mom put all the toys in a big yellow laundry basket and placed the basket in the closet. Krystal didn't get her toys back again for a whole day.

Krystal learned that if you do not take responsibility for the blessings you have in life, you may lose those blessings. Jesus taught that we are "in charge of the beast of the field." Jesus gives all that you have — your parents, your brothers and sisters, your home to live in and so many other wonderful things. If you are truly thankful for all that you have, then you will be a responsible person, and take good care of all that you have been given.

Your Turn

1. Why do you think Krystal didn't want to put her toys away?
2. What happened when Krystal wouldn't take care of her toys?
3. Have you ever had something taken away because you didn't take good care of it?

_____

_____

_____

Prayer

Thank You, Jesus, for all of the blessings in my life. Help me to always take good care of all of the wonderful things You have given me. Amen.

Make Your Own Toy Basket

Read this to your child: "Jesus wants you to be responsible and take good care of the things He gives you. Here is a basket you can make to help remind you how Krystal did not take care of her toys."

What You Need
• square-shaped piece of paper (construction paper or cardboard is best)
• crayons
• safety scissors
• tape

What to Do
Using the pattern as a guide, cut out on the solid lines and fold on the dashed lines. Fold up the sides and secure with tape.

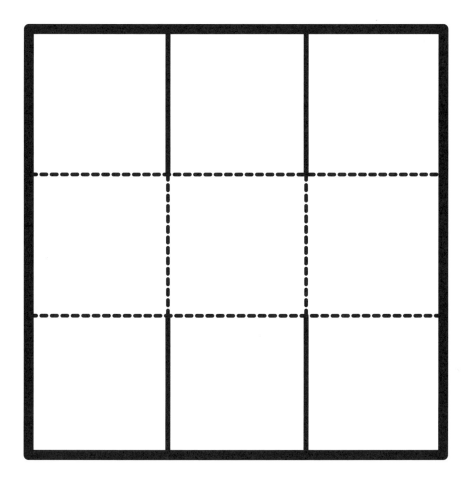

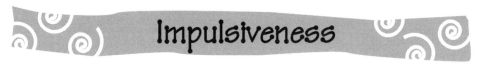

Impulsiveness

You should always think before doing something.
Let us be...self-controlled.
~1 Thessalonians 5:6

The Living Nativity

It was a cold, crisp December night when the entire family visited Grandma and Grandpa's church. The church was having a living nativity. The kids were very excited. As they walked through the tents they saw Roman soldiers, beggars, goats, sheep and even a camel.

But the most wonderful thing of all to Clare were the doves. They were snowy white and silky soft to touch. Clare loved them.

There was a lot to see in pretend Bethlehem, but finally they came to the best part. When they saw the stable where the baby Jesus lay in His mother Mary's arms, Clare couldn't take her eyes away. It was a beautiful, magical sight.

But then suddenly, Clare noticed something. There, in the back of the stable, on the very top of some stacked bales of straw, sat a dove. Clare dashed into the stable. Mom grabbed for her arm to stop her, but it was too late.

Before anyone knew what was happening, Clare had climbed to the top of the straw bales and was sitting next to the dove, happily petting his soft, white feathers. When "Joseph" climbed up to get Clare, Mom was embarrassed for Clare, and told Clare she shouldn't have done that.

Clare behaved impulsively. That means that she did something without thinking about it first. Clare wanted to pet the dove, so without even thinking whether she should, she did it.

Jesus doesn't want you to be impulsive. He wants you to think carefully before you do something. That way, you will be careful to live your life in a way that is best for you and others, according to God's will.

Your Turn

1. What did Clare do that she shouldn't have?
2. Why should you think first before you do something?
3. Can you remember a time when you did something you shouldn't have because you didn't think about it first?

_____

_____

Prayer

Please help me, Jesus, to think carefully before I choose to do something. I want to always behave in a way that would please You. Amen.

Find the Nativity

Read this to your child: "Jesus wants you to think carefully about what you do before you do it. Find your way to the nativity. Don't be distracted by all of the wonderful things along the way! When you are done, you can color the pictures."

Answer is on page 236.

Contentment

Jesus is always with you.
Let your gentleness be evident to all.
~Philippians 4:5

Arms of Contentment

Baby Anna was teething. That means her brand-new teeth were coming through her gums. It hurt her a lot. She usually liked to sleep by herself, but tonight she felt so hurt, scared and upset that she wanted to be near Mom. Mom lay down with Anna in bed and snuggled her close. Anna fidgeted at first, unable to settle down to sleep, so Mom cooed soft words of comfort in her ear and held her even tighter. The warmth of Mom's body, and the secure hold of her arms soon settled Anna into happy sleep.

For several hours, Mom and Anna lay there, snuggled tightly together and sleeping. From time to time Mom would wake for a moment to whisper, "Mom's here" or Anna would make a sweet baby-sound of happiness, but then they would fall back into dreamland.

Feeling safe, happy and loved is what contentment feels like — just like Mom and Anna felt as they snuggled together. Have you ever felt like that? You can feel contentment any time if you think about Jesus and how much He loves and cares for you. His love is like a mother's arms holding you gently as He shields you from harm.

Your Turn

1. Why was Anna upset?
2. What made Anna feel better?

_____

_____

_____

_____

_____

_____

Prayer

Thank You, Jesus, for Your love and care. I know that I can always feel safe and content with You. Amen.

Find Comfort

Read this to your child: "Jesus' arms are always around you. If you just remember how He cares for you, you can feel His love. Circle the items that bring people comfort. Draw an X over the things that don't make people feel better. Color the comforting pictures when you're done."

Answer is on page 236.

Gifts

God's gift of love is the greatest gift of all.
God so loved the world that he gave his one and only Son.
~John 3:16

Special Gifts

Brrr-ing, Brrr-ing, the phone rang. Who could it be? Gloria ran as fast as she could to answer it.

"Whom am I talking to?" asked Grandma. "Gloria?"

"Uh, yeah. Are you Grandma?" answered Gloria.

Gloria was so excited to hear Grandma's voice that she couldn't help but tell her about the special gift Daddy had just made. "Daddy made something for you," said Gloria. "It's a Jesus house, and it has people, too. I'm going to give it to you."

Daddy and Jonathan had made a wooden stable earlier that day for Grandma's nativity pieces. They had measured out each piece of wood with Daddy's tape measurer, carefully cut the wood with a saw, and Jonathan nailed each piece in place. They planned to give it to Grandma for Christmas. It was a special gift because they made it themselves out of love.

God also gave you a special gift of love. He gave you the greatest gift of all — salvation. It is because of Jesus that you are forgiven for your sins, and that's the most special gift of all.

Your Turn

1. What was Gloria so anxious to tell her grandma?
2. What made the stable a "special" gift?
3. What is the most special gift that there ever was?

_____

_____

_____

_____

_____

_____

Prayer

Thank You, Jesus, for Your "most special gift." It is because of You that my sins are forgiven. I love You. Amen.

Find the Gifts

Read this to your child: "Jesus gave the most special gift of all, but you can give gifts to others, too. Match the gift packages with the gift that is inside."

Surprise

God knows what's best for you.
In all things God works for the good.

~Romans 8:28

Surprise!

Matthew, Leanna and Sarah were very excited as they waited for their new baby brother or sister to come home. It seemed like such a long time since Mom and Dad had first told them that they were going to have a new baby in the house. They had asked over and over again when the baby would be born, but Mom always said "not yet." Finally one day Mom told them it was time for the baby to be born, and they were taken to Grandma and Grandpa's house. They were having lots of fun staying at Grandma's house, but they couldn't wait to meet the new baby. Even though they didn't know if the new baby would be a boy or a girl, they all agreed that it would be a boy.

They waited, and waited and waited for Daddy to call. When Daddy finally called from the hospital, they couldn't believe what he told them. How could it be? What a surprise! The new baby wasn't a boy at all. It was a girl! They all had expected a boy! When they saw their beautiful new baby Rachel, they found that it really didn't matter at all. They loved her just the same.

You probably won't always get what you expect. Sometimes God will surprise you with something other than what you want. Whatever God chooses for you, though, will always be the very best thing for you. You can always count on that.

Your Turn

1. Did Matthew, Leanna and Sarah want a brother or a sister?
2. How did the children feel when they saw they had a baby sister?
3. Were you ever surprised?

_____

_____

_____

_____

Prayer

Jesus, help me to always trust that You know what is best for me. Amen.

Choose Your Surprise

Read this to your child: "God's surprises are always good. Whatever He chooses for us is the best thing. Color the package. If you could open this package, what kind of a surprise would you like to find inside?"

 # Adventure

Doing new things can be scary as well as fun.
Be strong and courageous...the Lord...will be with you.

~Deuteronomy 31:7-8

Bath-Time Adventure

Ashley really wanted to take a bath with her big sister, Kelli. Every time Kelli took a bath, Ashley would stand at the edge of the tub watching. Sometimes Ashley even reached over the edge to dip her fingers in the warm, soapy water. Taking a bath in the big tub, with Kelli and all the tub toys, was just about the biggest adventure that Ashley could imagine. Adventures, however, while a lot of fun, can also be a little scary. Ashley wanted to go in the tub, but at the same time she was afraid to.

One day, as Kelli was taking her bath, Ashley couldn't stand it any longer. She decided then and there that she would go into the tub. She slowly lifted her leg over the side, but then put it back down. She fidgeted from foot to foot, trying to find the courage to go over the edge. Finally, she decided to set aside her fears and just dive into her great adventure, so she did.

With a loud splash, Ashley landed in the tub right next to Kelli. Kelli, seeing the bubbles all over her sister's face, giggled and asked, "Baby eat bubbles?" Kelli was delighted to share her bath with Ashley, and so was Ashley. Even though Ashley's clothes were soaking wet, and soap suds dripped off the end of her nose, she was very happy that she had begun her great bathing adventure.

Sometimes it can be hard to try new things. Doing new things is exciting and fun, but scary, too. If you trust in Jesus, you can, like Ashley, set your fears aside and begin wonderful adventures. Jesus will always be near you.

Your Turn

1. Why did Ashley want to go in the tub?
2. Why do you think Ashley was afraid to go in the tub?
3. Have you ever done something even though you were a little scared to do it?

_____

_____

_____

Prayer

Thank You, Jesus, for watching over me as I enjoy the many adventures of my life. Amen.

Bath Time Bubbles

Read this to your child: "If you trust Jesus, your fears will not stop you from having new adventures. Here is a new adventure you can have with blowing bubbles. The next time you are in the bathtub, or just playing outside, blow some bubbles — they're always lots of fun! You can use store-bought bubble mixture or the simple recipe here. Use slotted spoons to dip in the bubble mixture. Here are some bubbles to color."

What You Need
- 1/4 cup liquid dish detergent
- 1/2 cup water
- slotted spoons

What to Do
Mix and play!

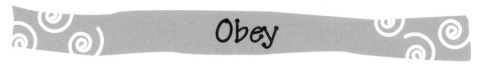

Obey

You must trust your parents to know what is best for you.
Honor your father and your mother.
~Exodus 20:12

Running Toward Danger

Francine loved to run away from Mom. Every time she had the chance, whether in a grocery store or just in the back yard, she dashed off.

One day, as Francine was playing with a ball out in the yard, she once again decided to run away. With all her strength, Francine threw her ball out into the road and then ran after it as fast as she could. Mom saw a bright red sports car zooming down the road toward Francine and cried out to her, "No, Francine! Stop!" but Francine didn't want to obey her mother. Francine just kept running, giggling all the way. She didn't understand that she was in danger. Mom ran after her as fast as she could and caught Francine just before she reached the road.

Have you ever disobeyed your mother or father? Jesus says to "honor your father and mother," which means that you should trust them and do what they tell you to do.

Francine didn't obey her mother. As a result, she almost got hurt very badly. You may not always understand the reasons why your parents tell you to do something, but just like you trust Jesus to know what is best for you, you must also trust your parents to know what is best for you.

Your Turn

1. What could have happened to Francine if she had run into the road?
2. Why should you always do what your parents, and Jesus, tell you to do?
3. Can you remember a time when you didn't obey your parents?

_____

_____

_____

_____

_____

Prayer

Thank You, Jesus, for the gift of parents who take care of me and teach me Your will. Amen.

Pressed Flowers

Read this to your child: "You cannot always understand everything Jesus or your parents tell you to do. But you should do it anyway. When Francine wants to do something wrong, her mom sometimes gives her something good to do instead. Then she forgets about doing the wrong thing. Sometimes Francine gets so busy collecting leaves, weeds and flowers that she forgets to run away from Mom. Why don't you try one of her favorite things to do? Just pick some leaves or flowers (or Francine's favorite: clover), place a sheet of waxed paper on top and below it, and slide it between two heavy books. Let it press for a couple of days."

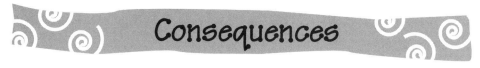

Consequences

Before making a choice, think about its consequences.
A man reaps what he sows.
~Galatians 6:7

Picking Trouble

There are always consequences for every choice. "Consequences" are the things that happen after you do something.

Beth knows about consequences. Every spring Mom plants flowers in planters on the back porch. This year, Beth got to help. Beth loved the bright colored flowers! There were orange marigolds, red begonias, white petunias and many more. Mom explained to her that the flowers were only for looking-at and that if Beth picked the flowers, she would not be allowed on the back porch again.

The next day Beth slowly reached out her hand and carefully touched the soft petals. They were so silky against her fingertips that she couldn't resist picking off the petals and rubbing them against her face and neck. It felt wonderful!

Maybe if I pick them very, very fast, she thought, *and just take the pretty part, Mom won't notice.* So Beth began picking the flowers as fast as she possibly could, leaving the stems behind.

She had almost finished picking all the flowers when her big sister, Camille, saw what she had done and yelled, "Beth's ruining all the flowers." After that, Beth wasn't allowed on the back porch again for a long time.

Beth knew what the consequences would be if she picked the flowers, but she chose to do it anyway. Just like Beth, you must make choices every day, and every choice you make causes something else to happen. That is why it is important to always think about the consequences of your choices before you decide what you want to do.

Jesus taught to always be very careful about what you choose, so you live the way He wants you to, instead of making choices that will hurt you.

Your Turn

1. Why did Beth want to pick the flowers?
2. What was the consequence of Beth picking the flowers (what happened to her after she did it)?
3. What would be your consequence if you picked flowers?

Prayer

Jesus, please help me to think about consequences before I make choices. Amen.

Color Your Own Flowers

Read this to your child: "If you are going to be a good Christian and live your life like Jesus wants you to, you must always think about the consequences of what you do. Beth still loves flowers, but now she colors them instead of picking them. There are lots of different kinds of flowers. Color these flowers with different colors."

"Now draw your own flower."

 # Celebration

Going to church shows Jesus that you love Him.
Sing to the Lord a new song.
~Psalm 149:1

Praise the Lord

"Do we have to go to church today?" asked Brenna. She and her sister both loved Sunday School and the children's sermon part of the church service, but found the rest of the service boring. It was hard for them to just sit quietly through all the songs and talking that they didn't understand.

Daddy explained to Brenna and Jill that they go to church to praise Jesus and to be with other people who love God. "It's a way for us to show Jesus how much He means to us," Daddy said. "And how much we appreciate all He does for us."

"But I don't know the songs," complained Jill. Mom told Jill that even though she doesn't know the words, she can still sing along by humming instead of singing the words.

"Jesus will understand that you're singing to praise Him even if you don't know the words," said Mom. "You know how much you like to hear me tell you I love you? Well, it makes Jesus happy, too, when He hears us praise Him. The words aren't really all that important, it's what we're feeling that counts."

Your Turn

1. Why didn't Brenna and Jill want to go to church?
2. Do you ever feel bored in church? Why?
3. Why do people to go church?

_____

_____

_____

_____

_____

_____

Prayer

Jesus, even though I don't always understand what is said in church, help me to remember that what is important is praising You. Amen.

What Are You Thankful For?

Read this to your child: "It is hard sometimes to understand the way adults praise Jesus, so why not praise Jesus in your own way? Have your mom or dad make a list of the things that you're thankful for in your life, then say a prayer thanking Jesus for all of the things on your list. You can draw pictures of what you are thankful for. Here are some ideas. You can color them if you like."

Deception

You should not deceive others.
The folly of fools is deception.

~Proverbs 14:8

Deceptive Kisses

"Audrey?" called Mom. "What are you doing?"

In a few seconds, Audrey peeked around the corner and said, "Playing," so Mom went back to work. Audrey dashed around the corner and into Mom's bedroom.

After a few more minutes, Mom once again called to Audrey. "Audrey? C'mon, I don't like you out of sight. What are you doing now?"

Audrey's mom suddenly saw her in the bedroom doorway. Audrey had a worried look on her face, and threw a bunch of kisses to Mom before she ran back into the bedroom. Now Mom knew something was up!

Mom quickly walked to the bedroom, and there was Audrey, sitting on the floor with Mom's nail polish bottles all around her. Mom had forgotten to put her box of polish away, and Audrey had deceived Mom long enough that she was able to get into it.

Audrey cleaned up the mess she had made. Then she and Mom had a long talk about the importance of honesty.

Deceiving someone is like lying to them, and it's very wrong. Audrey thought she could fool her mom by throwing her some kisses, but her plan didn't work. A disciple once tried to use a kiss to deceive Jesus. That disciple, Judas, thought that Jesus would think his kiss was out of love, when really it was a sign to the Roman soldiers to arrest Jesus.

Judas couldn't hide his deceptive behavior, and neither could Audrey. Just like Audrey, you may be able to deceive someone for a little while, but you can never deceive Jesus. He knows everything you do and say, and sees every sin. Therefore, you must try your best to only do what is good and right, and never deceive others just to have your own way.

Your Turn

1. Why did Audrey want to deceive her mom?
2. How was Audrey punished for her wrong action?
3. Can you ever fool Jesus? Why not?

Prayer

Please help me, Jesus, to remember that the same power that keeps me under Your care and guidance also makes You aware of my sins. I can never deceive You. Amen.

Count the Bottles

Read this to your child: "Jesus wants you to live an honest life, with love and caring for others. He does not want you to lie and deceive others. Audrey deceived her mom because she wanted to do something that was wrong. Here are the nail polish bottles that Audrey wasn't supposed to play with. Can you count how many of the bottles are the same, and how many look different? After you are done counting, color the bottles with your favorite nail polish colors."

Answer is on page 236.

Trust

Place your trust in Jesus for courage.
You will keep [him] in perfect peace...
because he trusts in you.

~Isaiah 26:3

Just Trust Me

"Just lie back and relax," Daddy said to Chad as they stood in the cool lake water. Chad didn't know how to swim. He was too scared to try.

Chad went into the lake many times each summer. He loved to splash around and feel the tiny fish nibble on his toes. He liked to watch those fish, and wished he could swim like them. But every time he tried to swim, Chad felt the water splashing on his face and got scared that he would sink deep under the water where he couldn't breathe.

"I won't let your face go under the water," said Daddy. "Just trust me."

Chad struggled with his fear but finally he lay back in the water. He could feel his dad's strong, warm hands holding up his body as he floated in the water. Daddy's strength gave him the courage to keep trying. Soon Chad was floating, and then paddling in the water all by himself.

Chad's trust in his Daddy gave him the courage to do something he was scared to do. In the same way, if you place your trust in Jesus, He will keep you safe and give you the strength to overcome your fears.

Your Turn

1. Of what was Chad afraid?
2. How did Chad's dad help him learn how to swim?
3. Do you remember a time when trusting someone helped you to not be afraid?

_____

_____

_____

_____

_____

Prayer

Jesus, please help me to remember to place my trust in You. Amen.

Find the Fish

The symbol of the cross reminds many Christians to put their trust in Jesus. A long time ago, however, before the symbol of the cross, the symbol of the fish was a way people showed each other that they were Christians. If you want to see what it looks like, color the sections that have the number 4 in them.

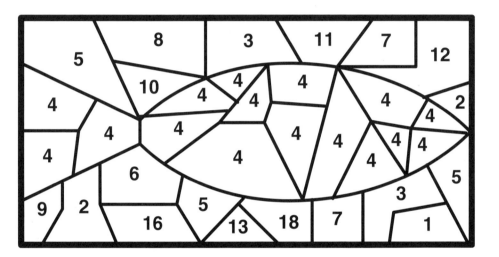

Answer is on page 236.

 # Reality

You should trust your parents and Jesus to teach
you what is important.
The word of the Lord is flawless.

~Psalms 18:30

What's Real?

Wendy sat on the floor in front of the TV, trying her best to win at her new video game. She was doing well, even though baby Claire was constantly reaching for the TV screen.

"She thinks they're real," explained Wendy to Mom as Claire squeaked and squealed at the little creatures dancing across the screen. "Claire's so silly," she laughed.

Wendy soon was more interested in watching Claire than she was in playing her video game. "Look, Claire," she said, pointing to the tiny video people. "Those aren't real. Those are just pictures."

Even though Wendy's explanation was clear and to the point, baby Claire still tried her best to capture the dancing video game figures. She grabbed to the left, then to the right, following the figures with wide, smiling eyes. She was having a lot of fun trying to catch them.

Like Claire, sometimes it can be hard to know what is real and what is not. When you are young there is so much you do not know yet that you need to depend upon the people who love you to help you. Claire had Wendy to teach her, you have your parents, and everyone has Jesus to teach what is real and important in life.

Your Turn

1. Why did baby Claire grab at the pictures on TV?
2. How did Wendy help Claire?
3. How do your parents help you to learn about life?

_____

_____

_____

_____

Prayer

Thank You, Jesus, for giving me people to love me and teach me about life, and thank You for all the guidance You give us all. Amen.

Real or Not Real?

Read this to your child: "Jesus is real. So are the things He teaches in the Bible. When it is hard to tell if something is real or not, you can trust Jesus and your parents to help you. Can you tell what is real and what isn't? Color the pictures, and then circle the 'real' things."

Answer is on page 237.

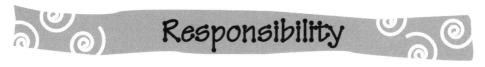

Responsibility

You should follow the rules because it is the right thing to do.
Each one should carry his own load.

~Galatians 6:5

Gina's Mess

Gina loves chocolate pudding. Mom cooked up a batch of it just for her and her brother, Billy. Now they were sitting at the kitchen counter happily enjoying its smooth, velvety texture and sweet, chocolate flavor. Yum, yum!

While they were still eating, Billy heard his favorite TV show starting. "Come on, Gina, our show is starting," Billy said as he picked up his plate and put it in the refrigerator. It was a strict house rule that no food could be left out on the table.

"I'm coming," called Gina as Billy ran to the living room. Popping one more spoonful of pudding in her mouth, Gina climbed down from her chair and ran after Billy, leaving her plate on the table.

Moments later, little Betsy appeared in the living room with chocolate pudding covering her face, clothes and hands. Gina had not obeyed the house rules, and now there was a big mess to clean up. Gina didn't take care of her responsibility before leaving to have fun, so she was punished by not being allowed to watch her show, and had to help clean up the mess Betsy made.

You should act responsibly simply because it's the right thing to do. Gina was not responsible. Jesus wants you to do your best in every way, including obeying the rules that your parents set for us.

Your Turn

1. Was Gina the only one who did something wrong?
2. Why is it important to be responsible and obey rules?
3. Do you always act responsibly?

_____

_____

_____

_____

_____

Prayer

Help me, Jesus, to always behave responsibly and obey the rules my parents, and You, have set for me. Amen.

Taking Responsibility

Read this to your child: "No matter what you are doing, Jesus wants you to take responsibility for the choices in your life. Color this picture of Gina taking care of one of her responsibilities."

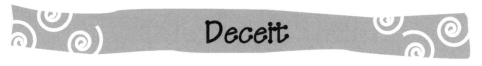

Deceit

You must place your faith only in Jesus.
He will make your paths straight.

~Proverbs 3:6

Steven Deceived

Shana pointed to the electrical outlet, trying to get baby Steven to play with it. She acted like she was going to touch it, then smiled and nodded as she pointed to it, as if she were saying, "It's okay," or "Do it, it's fun."

Shana knew that she wasn't allowed to play with the outlet. It was a house rule. But she would enjoy watching her cousin play with it if she could get him to do it.

Steven also knew that the outlets were never to be touched, but Shana convinced him to do it. Grabbing hold of the electrical cord, Steven yanked it out of the outlet. Just at that exact moment, Shana's mom saw what Steven did. He was scolded for doing something so wrong.

Steven had let himself be deceived by Shana. He knew that what he was doing was against the rules, but he did what Shana told him to instead. In the same way, people often allow themselves to be deceived by others, even when they know in their heart the right thing to do.

It can be easy to be fooled by other people. You must put your faith in Jesus and what you know is right, instead of putting your faith in other people.

Your Turn

1. Was Steven wrong?
2. Did Shana do anything wrong?
3. What should Steven had done when Shana wanted him to play with the outlet?

_____

_____

_____

_____

Prayer

Jesus, I want to always do what You tell me is right. Help me remember to trust only You. Amen.

Which Are Wrong?

Read this to your child: "The only thing in this world that you can have complete and total faith in is Jesus. He will never deceive you. You can trust Him to help you decide what is right or wrong. One of each of these pairs has something wrong with it. Don't be deceived — look carefully and circle the one that's correct. When you are done, color the picture."

Answer is on page 237.

Environment

You should take good care of the world God has given.
God...put him in the Garden of Eden to...take care of it.

~Genesis 2:15

Earth's Harvest

Madison sat in the tractor with Uncle Ken watching the corn stalks as they were sucked up into the cylinder to be harvested. The hard, yellow kernels of corn filled the grain bin behind them as they rolled along through the field.

Earlier that year in the spring, Madison and Daddy had driven the tractor through these same fields, loosening the dirt with the plow to get it ready for planting. Uncle Ken had planted the corn then, and all summer long Madison had watched as the corn grew from little sprouts, growing taller and taller with each passing day. It wasn't long until the corn was taller than Madison was! Now it was fall, and the corn Uncle Ken had planted was finally ripe. Helping Uncle Ken harvest the corn, Madison was once again playing an important part in taking care of the land God has given.

God made the earth and everything on it, and said that we should take good care of all the things He made. You should not be wasteful or destructive, but rather help our environment to stay healthy. Madison is doing her part to care for the earth. You can, too.

Your Turn

1. Why is it important to take good care of the earth?
2. What was Madison doing to care for the land?
3. How can you help to take care of this land God has given us?

_____

_____

_____

_____

_____

Prayer

Thank You, Jesus, for this wonderful planet Earth that You have given us. Please help me remember to take good care of the land that You have trusted to my care. Amen.

Where Did That Come From?

Read this to your child: "Do you know where your food comes from? Draw a line from the food you eat to the place it comes from.

Did you notice how Jesus is the center of everything? That's because Jesus made the world, and everything in it!"

Answer is on page 237.

Time

God wants you to use your time wisely.
There will be no more delay!
~Revelation 10:6

Scary Time?

It was late at night. The house was dark and quiet, except for eerie, strange sounds coming from the garage. Mom slowly got out of bed, careful to not make any noise. Slipping into her shoes, Mom crept silently to the back door leading to the garage. She could see light coming from the peephole and still hear the strange noises. Someone was in the garage!

Who, or what, could it be? Maybe it was a huge, hairy monster with big green eyes and long, sharp teeth! Maybe it was a burglar trying to steal the car! Who could it be? What was in the garage?

Mom peered through the peephole but couldn't see anyone or anything out of the ordinary, so as quietly as possible, Mom unlocked the door and opened it. Very, very slowly Mom opened the door, and, peeking around the corner, she finally saw where the noise was coming from. There at the workbench sat Dad with Brittany in her pajamas beside him. They were working on the lawn mower engine. Dad was carefully explaining what all the different parts were and what they did to make the mower work.

How you choose to spend your time is very important. God wants you to use everything He has given you, including time, in the very best way possible. Even though it was very late at night, Brittany and Dad were spending some special time with each other and learning something at the same time. For such a wonderful opportunity, it was okay to extend bedtime a little.

Your Turn

1. Who was making the "scary" sounds in the garage?
2. How were Brittany and Dad making good use of their time?
3. Has Mom or Dad every let you stay up late to do something fun or educational?

_____

_____

_____

_____

Prayer

Please guide me, Jesus, to use the time You have given me wisely. Amen.

What Is in the Garage?

Read this to your child: "Jesus wants you to spend time He gives you in the best way you can, and never waste it. Brittany and her dad found a way to do that. Find out what is in the garage. The door has already been opened for you. Color only the spaces that have the number 1 in them, and you'll see what's in our garage. What kind of things do you keep in your garage?"

Answer is on page 237.

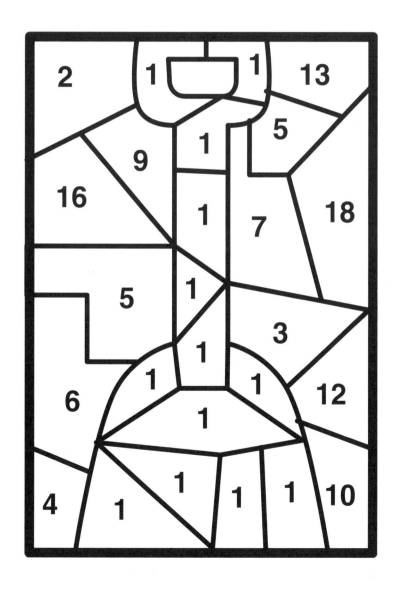

Courage

You can have courage because Jesus is always with you.
*Be strong and courageous...your God will be
with you wherever you go.*

~Joshua 1:9

Finding Courage

Tara really wanted to learn how to ride a bike, but she was scared to have Daddy let go of the bike while she was on it. Time after time Daddy put her on the bike and walked alongside her as Tara pushed on the peddles with her feet. Tara held onto the handlebars very tightly, carefully steering her bike down the gravel driveway, wiggling back and forth on the seat as she tried to balance. Sometimes Daddy tried to let go, but Tara would get scared and say, "Please, Daddy, hold on to me."

One day, after Daddy had helped Tara peddle up and down the driveway several times, Tara told him he could let go. Tara was still a little afraid, but because Daddy was beside her she found the courage to ride the bike on her own. Tara tipped her bike over a couple of times, but after some practice, she was riding on her own without falling over anymore.

Just like in Tara's story, you can have courage because you know that Jesus is always with you, holding onto you when you need Him to, or just walking beside you. Like Tara as she was learning to ride her bike, you may fall sometimes or make mistakes when you are learning something new, but Jesus will give you the courage to keep trying.

Your Turn

1. What was Tara afraid of?
2. Why wasn't Tara afraid when Daddy was next to her?
3. When was the last time that you did something even though you were afraid?

_____

_____

_____

_____

Prayer

Thank You, Jesus, for always walking beside me and keeping me safe from harm. Help me to remember that if I trust in You, I can find the courage to do anything. Amen.

Find Tara's House

Read this to your child: "Tara had courage because her dad believed in her. You can also have courage because Jesus believes in you. He helps you find your way in life. Now help Tara find her way through the maze to her house."

Answer is on page 237.

Faith

You feel faith in your heart, even though you cannot explain it.
Believe in the Lord Jesus.

~Acts 16:31

Having Faith

"Jesus made the whole world," said Hannah one day. She was watching a TV show about plants and how they grow.

"How do you know that Jesus made the whole world?" asked Mom. Mom was very proud of Hannah for knowing that Jesus made the world, but wondered how she would explain it.

Hannah smiled cleverly and answered, "He made the whole world with bears, and birds and giraffes, and more."

"It's true that Jesus made all of those animals, Hannah," said Mom. "But how do you know that He made them?"

Hannah looked frustrated now as she answered, "He made the whole world. He used His magic powers to make the world."

Hannah couldn't really explain how she knew that Jesus made the "whole world." She just knew. Faith is like that. It may be hard to explain the things that you learn in church and Sunday school. You believe in Jesus because the people you love and trust tell you about Him, and because you feel in your heart that it is right.

Your Turn

1. Who did Hannah say made the "whole world"?
2. Why did Hannah think that Jesus made the "whole world"?
3. Do you think that Jesus made the world and everything in it? Can you name some of the things that Jesus made?

_____

_____

_____

_____

_____

_____

Prayer

Thank You, Jesus, for giving me parents and the other people who love me to teach me about You. Amen.

What God Made

Circle the things that God made. When you are done, color the pictures.

Answer is on page 237.

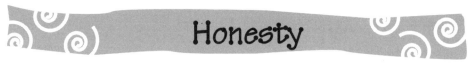

Honesty

You should tell the truth, even when you have done wrong.
Truthful lips endure forever.

~Proverbs 12:19

Who Took the Bread Dough?

"Did you take out the bread dough?" asked Mom. She had placed a batch of Treena's favorite bread dough in the refrigerator, and had told the children they shouldn't eat it. Now the bowl was setting out on the kitchen counter.

"No," Treena replied. "I didn't do it. Maybe Janet did it." Janet was watching cartoons in the next room, but looked up when she heard her name.

"I didn't do it!" Janet yelled. "Treena did it."

Treena looked guilty, so Mom asked her again, "Are you sure you didn't take the bread dough out?" Treena quietly looked at Mom but didn't answer.

"You know, Treena," Mom reminded her, "if you've done something bad you'll only make it worse by lying about it."

Treena was quiet a moment, then answered, "All I did was take it out. I didn't eat any. I know you said I couldn't eat any." Mom was disappointed in Treena for taking the bowl out, but proud of her for being honest. Because she was honest, Mom just talked to her about what she had done and didn't punish her.

Lies have a way of being found out even when you try your best to hide them. Lies do not get you out of trouble. Instead, lies make things worse. If you are honest when you do something bad, like Treena was, you at least admit your mistakes and you can say you are sorry. There is no sense in trying to hide your sins. After all, Jesus always knows the truth. You cannot hide from Him.

Your Turn

1. What did Treena do wrong?
2. Why did Treena lie?
3. Did Treena get in trouble when she told the truth?

Prayer

Dear Jesus, I'm sorry that I do bad things sometimes. Please help me to admit when I've done something wrong, so that I can be forgiven and not make the same mistake again. Amen.

Where Does the Bowl Go?

Read this to your child: "It is never OK to lie. Jesus always knows if you are telling the truth or not. Treena knows that now. Do you remember where the bowl of bread dough is supposed to be kept? Draw a line from the bowl to where it should go, then color the pictures."

Answer is on page 237.

Justice

Life isn't fair, but Jesus is.
Do not say, "I'll pay you back for this wrong!"
Wait for the Lord.

~Proverbs 20:22

Life Isn't Fair

"It's not fair!" yelled Evie as she stomped her feet. "I want to go to school, too."

"Look, Evie," said Travis, "you're not old enough to go to school. You're just little."

"I'm not little! I'm big. I'm very, very big," Evie said as she started crying. Travis had just started kindergarten, and Evie was sad that she wasn't going to school, too.

"Evie," explained Travis, "you don't even know your ABCs yet."

"Yes I do!" screamed Evie, stomping her feet again. "Mom," she yelled to the kitchen where Mom was cooking dinner, "Travis says I don't know my ABCs. Tell him I'm big!"

Mom explained to Evie that even though she was very big and very smart, the school's rules were that she had to be five years old to go, and that was a year away for Evie. Whether that was fair or not, those were the rules.

As Evie learned, life isn't fair. Sometimes bad things happen to good people, and sometimes rules may not make sense. The best you can do is try to live by the rules Jesus has given, and remember that when you go to heaven you will finally understand why things are the way they are.

Your Turn

1. Why was Evie upset?
2. Do you think it was fair that Evie couldn't go to school with Travis?
3. Can you think of some things that aren't fair?

_____

_____

_____

_____

Prayer

Jesus, please help me to put my trust in You even at times when life doesn't seem fair. Amen.

Are You Ready?

Read this to your child: "The world may not seem fair, but Jesus is. Evie is still learning that. Are you ready for school yet? Do you know your ABCs? Connect the dots below to trace the letters, then practice writing A-B-C by yourself."

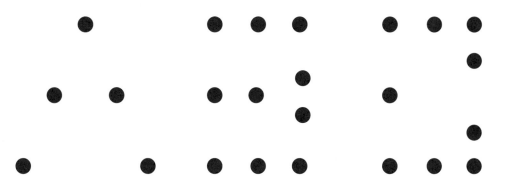

Answer is on page 237.

Prayer

You don't have to know a special prayer to talk to Jesus.
God has surely listened and heard my voice in prayer.

~Psalm 66:19

All Prayers Are Special

"Did you remember to say your prayers?" Mom asked as Ginny was tucked into bed for the night.

"I can't," answered Ginny. "I don't know how."

"What do you mean?" asked Mom.

"I don't know the words," said Ginny. "You have to say it." Ginny thought she could only say a certain kind of prayer to Jesus.

Mom said Ginny's prayers with her, and then explained, "Jesus doesn't mind if you don't know a special prayer. He just wants to hear from you. You can tell Him anything you want."

"Can I tell Him I'm Ginny?" she asked.

"Of course you can," answered Mom. "You can tell Him all about your day, how much you love Him, and it would be nice if you thanked Him for everything He's given us. Jesus loves you and He loves when you talk to Him."

Ginny learned something important about Jesus that night. She learned that she can talk to Jesus about anything, just like a good friend. You can also talk to Jesus whenever you want. Prayers are not only for nighttime. You can talk to Jesus at any time of the day or night. He is always there for you.

Your Turn

1. Why didn't Ginny say her prayers by herself?
2. What kinds of things does Jesus like for you to pray about?
3. What prayers do you say at bedtime?

_____

_____

_____

_____

_____

Prayer

Thank You, Jesus, for letting me say anything I need to when I pray to You. Amen.

Write Your Own Prayer

Read this to your child: "Ginny learned that Jesus does not care how fancy or perfect your prayers are, as long as whatever you say comes from your heart. Make up your own special prayer to Jesus, and have your mom or dad help you write in the words. Here is a little help to get you started. Just fill in the spaces."

Dear Jesus, I love You very much. Thank You for loving me, too. My favorite thing that happened today was_____. Thank You for_____. Please always keep me safe, and take extra special care of_____. Bless all of the important people in my life, but especially Mommy, Daddy, _____&_____. Amen.

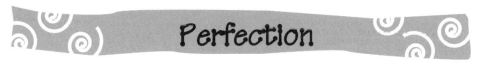

Perfection

You do not have to be perfect.
Love covers over a multitude of sins.

~1 Peter 4:8

The Perfect Baby

The Perfect Baby was born in November, long before Christmas, but still the best present her family received that year. She was soft and pink, and perfect. She was named Rachel because her parents liked the story of Rachel in the Bible, and they hoped she would someday like it and learn from it, too.

Baby Rachel never cried or fussed for long. She often slept through the night. She was snugly and wonderful. She was every parent's dream. Rachel was so wonderful, in fact, that her parents nicknamed her "The Perfect Baby."

Through the first months of her life, baby Rachel continued to live up to her nickname, but as she grew old enough to move around on her own, she started to get into trouble. Several times she scooted off with her mom's table doilies. More than once she yanked on her brother's video game cords or dragged his video tapes off into another room. She even dug her tiny fingers into her mom's potted plant, spilling dirt all over herself and the carpet.

Her brother asked if perhaps Rachel should not be called The Perfect Baby anymore, but her mom and dad still did. To Rachel's parents it didn't matter what baby Rachel did because in their eyes Rachel and her brother were always perfect, just because they were theirs and they loved them so much.

You do not have to be perfect. Love does not demand that you never make a mistake or always do the right thing. Just like Rachel and her parents, Jesus sees you as you really are, with all of your faults, yet He still loves you more than you can understand. That is the way love is. That is the way Jesus is. You never need to worry that you will not be good enough for His love. His love is for always, and you are always "perfect" in His eyes.

Your Turn

1. Why was Rachel nicknamed "The Perfect Baby"?
2. Why did everyone continue to call Rachel "perfect" even when she did wrong things?
3. When you love someone, does it matter if he or she is perfect or not?

Prayer

Jesus, thank You for always loving me and seeing the best in me. Please help me to love others in the same way. Amen.

Find What's Wrong

Read this to your child: "You don't have to be perfect for Jesus to love you. He loves you even when you do bad things. Draw an X over the wrong things that Rachel did. Circle the nice things about Rachel."

Answer is on page 237.

Punishment

Punishment may feel bad, but it is a good thing.
God disciplines us for our good.
~Hebrews 12:10

The Gift of Punishment

What a terrible sight! Olga was sitting by the gerbil aquarium, holding a bag of gerbil food in her hands and munching away. She had been told many times that she was not to eat her pet gerbil's food, but she did it anyway.

After checking with the doctor, Mom scolded Olga for doing such a bad thing, and then put her in the time-out corner. Olga didn't like to be in the corner. She started to cry.

No one likes to be punished. It is not fun. But punishment is a very important thing. It helps you to be a better person. When Olga was punished she learned that breaking the rules causes something bad to happen. It was an important lesson for her to learn. Hopefully she will remember how much she disliked the punishment and never eat gerbil food again.

Jesus was also punished in a very important way. He loved you so much that He let Himself be punished for something He didn't even do. That is why Jesus died on the cross. He died to save you from your sins so that you wouldn't have to take that punishment yourself. That is how much He loves you.

Your Turn

1. What did Olga do that was wrong?
2. What did Olga learn from her punishment?
3. When was the last time you were punished? What did you learn from it?

_____

_____

_____

_____

_____

Prayer

Thank You, Jesus, for Your very important gift of punishment. Help me to learn the lessons that it teaches me. Amen.

What Goes Together?

Read this to your child: "Jesus gave the gift of punishment to help people learn and keep everyone safe. Olga did not understand that gerbil food is not the same as people food. She needed to learn that some things do not go together. Draw a circle around the pictures in each box that go together. When you are done, color the pictures."

Answer is on page 237.

Family

Family is more important than material things.
Children are a reward from him.

~Psalm 127:3

More Babies!

"When are we going to have another baby?" asked Abby.

Mom looked surprised as she answered, "We're not sure we're going to have another baby." Abby was used to either having a new baby to play with, or having one on the way. She had two sisters already, and she was the oldest.

"Jillian's almost a whole year old now," explained Abby. "She's not a baby anymore. When are you going to start growing another baby?"

Mom thought about Abby's question for a minute, then answered, "I'm not sure I can take care of another baby right now, Abby, or if we even have enough money to raise another child. I need you girls to get a little older before I think about having another baby."

Abby looked very serious as she said, "Look, Mom, I'm a lot older now and I can take care of the babies, so you can have another one." Abby went on to offer to share her toys, let the baby sleep in her room and baby-sit all of the time. She loved babies.

Abby knew the value of family. Just as Jesus teaches, you should value people more than things. Abby did not mind sharing her room and her toys, or giving her time to take care of her sisters. She would rather have another little brother or sister.

Your Turn

1. What did Abby want her mom to do?
2. If Abby could chose between having another baby, or a room full of new toys, which do you think she would choose?
3. Why does Jesus want you to value people more than material things?

_____

_____

_____

_____

Prayer

Thank You, Jesus, for the precious gift of family to love and share my life with. Please help me to remember that no matter how wonderful my toys and other things are, people are far more important. Amen.

Connect the Dots

Read this to your child: "Jesus teaches to value people more than things. Abby knows the importance of family and that is why she wants more babies. Connect the dots to complete each number, then match the babies with the correct number."

Answer is on page 237.

Manners

Good manners are important.
*The good man brings good things out of
the good stored up in him.*

~Matthew 12:35

Give Me Some Privacy!

Melanie was changing her clothes. She didn't like the blue jeans and T-shirt that Mom had put on her. She wanted to wear her soft, pink pants and fuzzy, purple shirt with the picture of a ballerina on it. As she began to change into her clothes, her big brother, Russell, came into the room.

"Get out!" screamed Melanie. "I'm changing my clothes. Give me some privacy!"

Russell didn't want to leave the room. He came in to play, and couldn't understand why his sister wanted him to leave.

"Give me some privacy!" Melanie yelled again. She was mad that Russell would not leave.

"I want to play with the blocks," Russell said. "I'm not leaving."

Melanie screamed again and Mom came in to explain to Russell that leaving the room when someone is changing clothes is good manners, and he should have left when his sister asked him to.

Good manners are not always easy to understand, and can be hard to remember sometimes. However strange it may seem, things like sitting up straight at the dinner table, taking turns on the playground, and saying "please" and "excuse me" are very important. Jesus wants you to show people that you care about yourself and others. Good manners does that.

Your Turn

1. What did Russell do that was rude?
2. Why are good manners important?
3. Is it hard to have good manners sometimes?

_____

_____

_____

_____

Prayer

Thank You, Jesus, for loving me and showing me every day that You care about me. Help me to show others that I care about them, too, by using good manners. Amen.

What Is Polite?

Read this to your child: "Jesus wants you to care about yourself and others. Good manners do that. What would be the polite thing to do in each of the following situations? After discussing your answers, color the pictures."

Guidance

The light of Jesus' love guides us every day.
Make straight your way.

~Psalm 5:8

Let God Light Your Way!

Rex watched TV while Emma happily turned the pages in her picture book. In the next room, Mom worked on the computer as the sun slowly set in the sky behind her.

Suddenly the lights went out, the TV went silent and the computer's steady hum died down to nothing. The electricity was out! Rex and Emma were worried. It got darker and darker, and soon they couldn't see at all. The silent darkness surrounded them like a heavy blanket. They started to get scared.

Mom quickly looked for flashlights, but both that she found needed new batteries and did not work. Then she remembered the candle in the china cabinet. Carefully feeling around the fancy dishes, Mom found the candle and matches. As the bright flame of the match lit, the room seemed to burst into light.

The warm glow of the candle's light comforted Rex and Emma, and they were no longer afraid. Even though the electricity was out for several hours, the candle lit their night beautifully while they were awake, and was a soothing night light as they slept.

Just like the candle lit Rex and Emma's way in the darkness, Jesus lights your way through life with His love and wisdom. When you are scared or worried, Jesus comforts you. When you cannot find your way, the light of Jesus' love guides you. You should be thankful for His light in your life, and accept the guidance He offers.

Your Turn

1. Why were Rex and Emma afraid?
2. What happened that stopped Rex and Emma from being afraid?
3. Can you remember a time when you felt afraid? What made you feel better?

_____

_____

_____

Prayer

Please help me, Jesus, to remember that You are always by my side, so I never need to be afraid. Amen.

What Goes Together?

Read this to your child: "If you know Jesus' will, it can be easier for you to find your way in life. In the same way, Rex and Emma's mom knew how to find the candle even in the dark because she knew that her candles are always kept in the china cabinet. Can you tell which things go together in the boxes below? Circle the things in each box that should go together."

Answer is on page 237.

 # Warmth

The warmth of Jesus' love is always with you.
The Lord Almighty is with us.
~Psalm 46:11

Special Kinds of Warmth

Everyone has a way to get warm when they are cold or scared. The Ward kids are no different.

Brett Ward's favorite spot in his house during the winter is a heat duct. This is where the heat blows out from the floor. When Brett hears the furnace turn on, he runs for the nearest duct and huddles beside it. Sometimes he lets the heat blow up under his shirt, giggling as the soothing air tickles his skin.

Caitlin and Fay warm up in a different way. They like to curl up in Mom or Dad's lap and snuggle. Nothing makes them happier than to feel strong arms around them, and hear loving words whispered in their ears.

Julia's favorite way to warm up is by cuddling in her own special blanket. Grandma gave it to her when she was just a baby. It is soft and pink, and it is the perfect way to warm up on a cool day. It can even make her feel better when she is sad or scared. Her blanket gives her a special kind of warmth.

Another special kind of warmth comes from Jesus. This warmth is much softer, soothing and far more comforting than anything else. Jesus' love warms you when you are cold and wraps around you like a protective blanket when you are afraid. You can feel His arms around you like a concerned parent even in your most difficult times. No warmth will ever be as satisfying or lasting than the special warmth of Jesus' love for you.

Your Turn

1. Where is Brett's favorite place to get warm?
2. Why is the warmth of Jesus' love better than anything else?
3. Will Jesus' love ever end?

_____

_____

_____

_____

Prayer

Thank You, Jesus, for the special warmth of Your love that is always with me. Amen.

What Makes You Feel Better?

Read this to your child: "Thinking about Jesus' love for you can always make you feel warm and comforted. Circle the other things that make you feel better when you are cold or sad, then color the pictures."

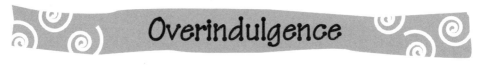

Overindulgence

Too much of a good thing can be bad.
Eat just enough — too much of it, and you will vomit.
~Proverbs 25:16

Enough Is Enough

"Not too fast kids," Mom warned. Leanna's godfather had come for a visit with his wife and baby daughter, Caroline. Caroline was in a baby walker. She was too little to make it move by herself, so she was very happy to have Matthew and Leanna push her around in it.

"Be careful," Mom continued. "If you push Caroline too fast, she could get scared."

"I won't scare her," said Leanna and off she ran, pushing Caroline in front of her. Lovely baby Caroline squealed with joy as she zoomed down the hallway in the walker. Over and over Leanna and Matthew took turns pushing her, and again and again Caroline squeaked and giggled her happiness over their little game.

The three children happily continued their fun for quite some time, but soon Caroline stopped laughing. Mom warned that the baby might be getting tired of their game, and that they should stop, but Matthew and Leanna kept going. Up and down the hall they raced, over and over again, until finally Caroline started to holler. She had liked being pushed, but now it was too much. Too much movement, too much noise and just too much fun. Caroline started to cry.

Too much of something good can actually make it seem bad. Most things are better if you do not get too much of them. For example, just think how sick you might get if you never ate anything but candy, or stayed up all night long every night! Jesus wants you to have fun and enjoy all of the blessings He has given you, but you also need to know when enough is enough.

Your Turn

1. How were Matthew and Leanna playing with Caroline?
2. Why did Caroline start to cry?
3. Can you think of some other things that are wonderful in small amounts, but not as nice if you have too much of them?

Prayer

Thank You, Jesus, for all of the wonderful things You have given us. Please help me to remember that too much of a good thing is not really good at all. Amen.

What Scares You?

Even good things can be scary sometimes. What kinds of things scare you? Draw a line under the pictures you think are scary, then color them. Remember that Jesus makes all good things but you have to know when good things are bad and stay away from them.

Violence

Bad things happen, but you can trust Jesus.
Open my eyes that I may see wonderful things.

~Psalm 119:18

A Violent World

"Why did that man hurt the little girl?" asked Preston. He had just seen part of the evening news about a man who kidnapped a little girl from a shopping mall.

Mom held Preston in her arms as she told him, "I'm not sure, Preston. He did a very bad thing, that's clear. But why people do bad things isn't always as clear."

"But why?" asked Preston again. He was trying hard to understand.

"Well, Preston," Mom began, "some people do bad things just because they want to, because they only think about themselves and don't care about other people's feelings. Other people do bad things because they are sick inside. There are a lot of reasons."

Mom gave Preston a big hug as she continued, "I know it's hard to understand, but bad things happen all the time, that's just the way the world is. Jesus brings a lot of joy and love into our world, but there's always evil here too, so we must do our best to guard against it."

When bad things happen it can be scary. Even though it is hard to understand why bad things happen, you need to trust in Jesus to know what is best for you and the world around you.

Your Turn

1. What did Preston want to know?
2. Why do you think people do bad things sometimes?
3. Why should you trust Jesus?

_____

_____

_____

_____

_____

Prayer

Dear Jesus, please help people to not do bad things. Protect me from the evil in the world. Amen.

Bad or Good?

Read this to your child: "Even when bad things happen, you must trust Jesus to know what is good for you and your world. Draw an X through the things that are bad, and circle the ones that are good. When you are done, color the pictures."

Answer is on page 237.

Answers

page 15

page 21

page 39

page 45

page 49

page 57

page 61

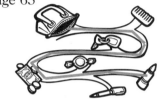

page 63

page 65

page 69

page 75

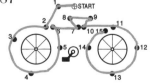

page 87

page 89

235

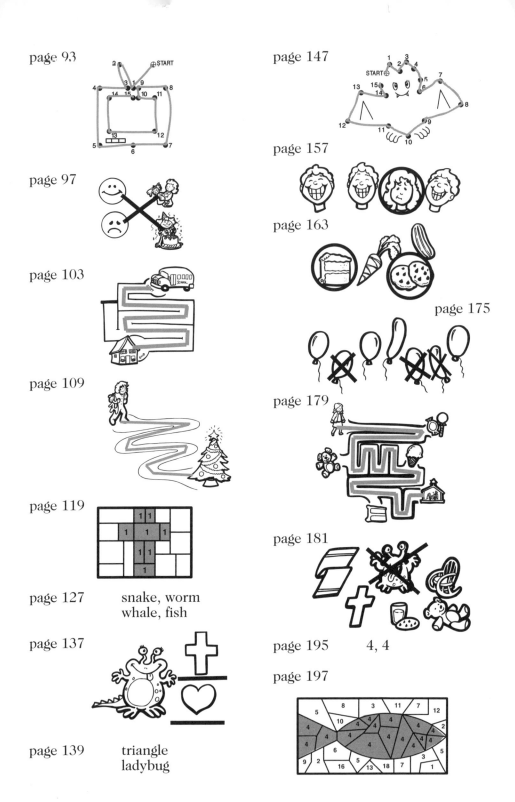

page 93

page 97

page 103

page 109

page 119

page 127   snake, worm
whale, fish

page 137

page 139   triangle
ladybug

page 147

page 157

page 163

page 175

page 179

page 181

page 195   4, 4

page 197

page 199

page 203

page 205

page 207

page 209

page 211

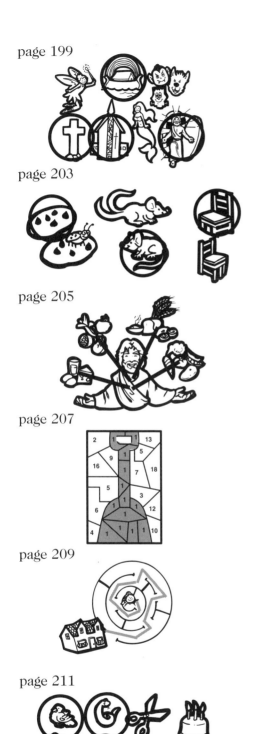

page 213

page 215

page 219

page 221

page 223

page 227

page 233

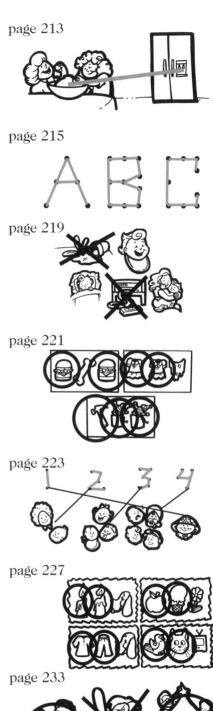

New!

L48220

THE GIRL'S GUIDE TO LIFE

Ages 10–12, 192 pages, Paperback, Illustrated.
The Girl's Guide to Life is for girls who want a road map to lead them through life's journey. *The Girl's Guide to Life* points to the Bible, the best map of all, talks about issues girls face like family, friends, boys, school, money, nutrition, fitness, and standing firm when temptations appear. Ages 10–12.

THE CHRISTIAN GIRL'S GUIDE FOR PRETEENS

Ages 10–12, 176-208 pages, Paperback, Illustrated.
Encourage girls with these fun and creative books covering issues that matter most to preteens: fashion, being their best, making friends, understanding the Bible, getting along with Mom, dealing with money, and LIFE! Ages 10–12.

L48213

L48211

L48212

L48213

L48214

L48215

L48216

L48217

L48218

L48219

GOD'S GIRLS Fun Crafts Plus Devotions!

Ages 9–12, 184 pages, Paperback, Illustrated. Preteen girls will be captivated by this book, with devotions about Biblical women and crafts created especially for girls. Weaving belts, decorating rooms and party planning activities all teach girls that fun and faith are part of God's plan. Ages 9–12.

L48011

THE GOD AND ME!® BIBLE

Ages 6–9, 192 pages, Paperback, Full Color Illustrations. Designed to capture the vivid imaginations of growing girls, The God and Me! Bible puts God's Word inot the hearts and minds. The bright illustrations, creative activities, puzzles, and games that accompany each Bible story make learning important Bible truths both fun and easy. Ages 6–9.

L48522

JUST FOR ME! FOR GIRLS

Ages 6–9, 152 pages, Paperback, Illustrated.
Through Stories, crafts, and fun activities, younger girls will discover what they need to grow closer to God! Ages 6–9.

L48413

L48412

L48411

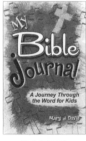

L46911

DB46731

GUIDED JOURNALS FOR GIRLS AND BOYS

Ages 10–12, 136–160 pages, Paperback, Illustrated. Preteen boys and girls will love these daily devotional journals that really encourage them to dig into the Bible.

Find more great stuff by visiting our website: **www.Rose-Publishing.com**